IS BARACK OBAMA'S BIRTH CERTIFICATE A FRAUD?

IS BARACK OBAMA'S BIRTH CERTIFICATE A FRAUD?

A Computer Guy Examines the Evidence for Forgery

John Woodman

NEW HORIZON PRESS

Published by New Horizon Press, 3509 E Linwood Dr, Springfield MO 65809

Publisher's Cataloging-in-Publication Data

Woodman, John.
    Is Barack Obama's birth certificate a fraud? : a computer guy examines the evidence for forgery / John Woodman.
    p. cm.
    Includes bibliographical references.
    ISBN 978-0-9837592-5-6
    1. Obama, Barack. 2. Birth certificates – Hawaii. 3. Birth certificates – Forgeries – Hawaii. 4. Presidents – Legal status, laws, etc. – United States. I. Title.

E908.3 .W66 2011
973.932—dc23   2011910692

Printed in the United States of America

10 9 8 7 6 5 4 3 2 1

*Thanks to my wife Joan,
to our children,
and to those who gave advice and help
whether editorial or technical –
Larry & Joanne Burrows, Vern Reeder,
Marilyn McCroskey, and Raegan Wiechert*

TABLE OF CONTENTS

A BIRTH CERTIFICATE ON TRIAL

About a week before Barack Obama suddenly released his long-form birth certificate to the world, I was jotting down some notes for a letter to the editor of the local newspaper.

I was going to express my opinion that the American people's skepticism of Obama's eligibility to the Presidency was the fault of none other than Barack Obama himself, and of those around him.

For more than two years, I felt, the standard response had been to marginalize those who dared to ask for real proof that their President was eligible to hold that office. Such questions seemed generally to be dismissed either with a wave, with a flat assertion that the question had already been answered – or even worse, with a snicker.

There was even an uncomplimentary label for people who asked such questions: *"birther."*

I didn't necessarily consider myself a "birther," but like a huge number of Americans, I did have some questions. And, I had significant doubts. I might have labeled myself a bit of an "eligibility skeptic." Like many Americans, I had hoped Barack Obama would release his long-form birth certificate, and I was puzzled as to why he hadn't done so.

1

1 – Barack Obama's Long-Form Birth Certificate (Official PDF)

When the long-form certificate was officially released, in the form of a PDF file[1] on April 27, 2011,[2] I was fascinated by the immediate flood of accusations that it was a fake. I was also interested in finding out the truth for myself.

It was this interest to get to the bottom of the mess, to work out the truth, that led me to dig deep into the allegations – just to see if any of them could really be sustained. A lot of the questions were computer related. So as a computer guy, I felt right at home.

And the issues seemed pretty darn important. If any of the claims of forgery could be proven, it would mean that a crime of fraud had been committed, and that the President of the United States was in all likelihood ineligible to hold the most powerful and important office in the world.

And since the certificate contains an apparently legitimate signature by Mr. Obama's mother – I had compared this closely with known signatures available online[3] – then active, direct and personal cooperation in the fraud would almost certainly have had to come from the one person in the White House who would've had access to a never-before seen authentic signature from Stanley Ann Dunham Obama: *Barack Obama himself.*

In the weeks after the release, I analyzed and did research every time a new question arose. And I did my own independent examination of the document itself. I found that in many cases where critics claimed an absolute proof of forgery, the "proof" quickly fell apart upon close examination.

Some of the weaker arguments, frankly, seemed a bit of an embarrassment. For example, quite a few people had never encountered the term "Certificate of Live Birth" as official language for a "birth certificate." And some of these, rather than check out the facts, had decided to claim that the document was completely invalid simply because it didn't come with their preferred label.

As a political conservative, I felt that some of the less informed arguments and theories reflected badly upon my side of the aisle.

After a month or so, I realized I had enough knowledge about the issue to make a significant contribution to the public conversation. And that's how this book was born.

An Emotionally Charged Issue

It didn't take long for me to realize that many people felt passionately about the issue, one way or another. Some who had come to believe that Mr. Obama was probably born outside of the United States seemed eager to embrace the latest "proofs of fraud," and reluctant to let go even of theories that were very clearly wrongheaded.

After seeing several of the new theories rack up hundreds of thousands of views on YouTube, I posted a few videos of my own.[4] As that series of videos progressed, the ratio of "dislikes" to "likes" went up. Apparently some who watched were unhappy with the fact that I was disproving some popular theories that they wanted to believe.

On the other hand, there were other YouTube users who wrote to thank and encourage me for giving an honest view of the issues.

I felt then, and I feel now, that whatever side of the political spectrum you might be on, it's better to know the truth. When you're out in the woods, a compass and a map are always useful – no matter whether they show that you're close to your campsite, or far out in the wilderness, somewhere that you may not particularly want to be.

How to Get to the Truth

Quite a few people, it seems, would like either to discredit the "birthers," or to discredit Mr. Obama.

My goal was a little bit different: it was to sort through all of the arguments and see what made sense.

As I see it, there are two basic ways of coming to a decision on what to believe about any particular issue.

Here's one method – and it's a really popular one: First, decide (whether consciously or unconsciously) what you *want* to believe.

Then, look for evidence to support that belief.

Now this is how a lot of folks like to make decisions, and this method definitely has some advantages. It allows you to freely *choose* you beliefs. Freedom!

The problem with freely choosing your beliefs, though, is that it often leads to believing things that just aren't true. And there are usually disadvantages (sometimes big ones) to believing things that aren't in line with the way things actually are.

A second method is to try and keep an open mind, to be *aware* of the things you'd rather believe, but to be willing to let go of those beliefs – *if* you find that facts and reason lead you to a different conclusion.

This is admittedly more difficult, because it means that you have to give up a certain amount of control over what you're going to believe. Your beliefs are no longer up to you. They're formed by the facts of the situation. And you can't control the facts.

Changing one's beliefs has consequences.

Our entire lives are built upon our beliefs. A shift in beliefs – especially major ones – can cause all kinds of upheaval. And for some of us, it simply isn't worth it. We find it much better to retreat back to the comfort of our *preferred* beliefs.

And I understand this – or at least think I do. But long ago, I decided that I would rather do my best to let the facts dictate what I believe, instead of choosing those beliefs in advance and then holding on no matter what.

The benefit, I find, is a closer harmony with reality. And I believe that being close to reality enables us to better deal with it. It's all to do with having an accurate map.

So if it's the truth we want to get to, then we need to start without a commitment to any particular conclusion. We must be willing to find out things we may not want to find out. This applies no matter what side of the political spectrum we're on.

Or, to put it another way: We can't reach the truth simply by assuming that the things we want to prove are true – or by resisting any discovery that they aren't. To resist a close examination of what we want to believe is only to "protect" ourselves from the light of reality.

Nor are we likely to get to the truth by failing to dig deep enough, by brushing aside bits of evidence we don't really want to hear, or by dealing with the issues only on a superficial level.

On the other hand, *if* our beliefs will stand up under the harshest interrogation we can give them, then they will probably hold up under others' interrogation as well. And we will know that what we believe is truly on solid ground.

And there's a lot of benefit in being able to be confident in your beliefs.

It was in this spirit, then, that I started my exploration.

All We Need Is One Good Proof

I began under the personal assumption that Barack Obama had been dodging the issues – and that therefore he probably either had not been born in the United States as he claimed, or there was something else regarding his long-form birth certificate that he didn't want revealed.

However, having a suspicion and really proving it are two different things.

Many people have claimed to prove things regarding Obama's birth certificate. By my estimation, the long-form birth certificate has been ruled a forgery or invalid on more than three dozen different counts. Some of these are trivial. Others are a bit harder to answer.

When you have a long list of accusations to deal with, there are two different levels at which you will eventually need to make decisions regarding the evidence.

The first has to do with each individual item of evidence.

We can and will look at all of the major clues as to whether or not the document is a forgery; and in dealing with each issue, we will decide whether or not the evidence seems compelling.

Once we've done that, we have some *overall* conclusions to reach. Here are some of the broader questions:

1. In the end, do we have compelling evidence that the document is a forgery?

2. Overall, do we have compelling evidence that Mr. Obama is ineligible to be President?

3. Are there more questions that could or should or might be investigated?

In order to prove a forgery, we don't have to have two or three or ten different arguments that will stick. All we need is *one single irrefutable proof*.

And we will do our best to find such a proof. If we can't find one, though, we won't be allowed by the rules of honest investigation to manufacture it – because "manufacturing proof" doesn't lead to establishing the truth.

On the other hand, if we should find that we are able to safely dismiss every single claim of forgery that has been made so far, doing so won't guarantee the authenticity of Barack Obama's long-form birth certificate. A document might pass every test we can test it with, and still be a fake.

However, by taking a hard look at the document, we will *definitely* be able to learn a great deal about it. And the end result should certainly be to advance the conversation on the topic.

Please Don't Shoot the Messenger!

I hope you understand by now that my purpose, to the extent possible, is to give the document and the various theories a fair, detailed, clear-headed, careful examination.

Our major goal is to unravel a mystery. That doesn't mean I'm necessarily going to try and keep this book completely free of any political commentary. I have my own views, and knowing what those are will likely better help you, the reader, to put the book in context. But I will try and keep such commentary to a minimum.

So that you may know, though, please allow me to state up front: I am *not* a supporter of Mr. Obama or his policies.

In my view, the "liberal" desire to try and "meet the needs" of every single American is driving our country steadily towards the edge of the cliff. And when we can no longer afford to pay the interest on what amounts to our maxed-out national credit card, it won't be just the wealthy who suffer from the resulting bankruptcy. It will be seniors, single parent families, everyone who currently receives government assistance of any kind, and ultimately, just about every single one of us.

End of lecture.

Whether you are conservative or liberal, you will probably find a few things in this book that you don't like. And the opposite is true as well. Whatever your views, I will probably say a few things that you *can* approve of.

I hope you will judge this book on the basis of my attempts to uncover the truth and provide useful information, rather than on anything I might say that you just don't like.

Regarding any Errors

If I have genuinely made a mistake in any of my investigations, I'll do my best to correct it in any future editions.

So if you sincerely believe you can show I've made an error, please email me at: *obamabook@springfieldcomputerguy.com*. I can't guarantee a response, but I'll do my best to make whatever corrections I can.

More Information

Additional information and updates may be available through: *www.ObamaBirthBook.com*.

A PARADE OF REPORTED EXPERTS

It's been reported that "many experts" have looked at Barack Obama's long-form birth certificate and declared it a fraud.[5]

A specific "cast of characters" are known either to have evaluated the document, or promoted theories to the public. The most prominent of these are the following:

Dr. Jerome Corsi

Jerome Corsi is the author of the best-selling book, *Where's the Birth Certificate? The Case That Barack Obama Is Not Eligible to Be President.*

Dr. Corsi is a senior writer for the popular web site *WorldNetDaily*, which brings his work to several million visitors every month. He has written at least two previous best-selling books. He holds a Ph.D. in political science from Harvard University. [6,7]

In addition to writing *Where's the Birth Certificate?* and regular articles for *WorldNetDaily*, Dr. Corsi has made numerous media appearances across the country, reportedly doing as many as 20 radio shows a day in regard to his book. Along with other questions regarding Barack Obama's eligibility, he has widely promoted the idea that the PDF file released by the White House is a fraud.

It would not be an exaggeration to describe Dr. Jerome Corsi as a driving force, if not *the* driving force, behind Americans' doubts regarding Mr. Obama's eligibility to the Office of President.

Karl Denninger

Karl Denninger is the founder of *market-ticker.org*. He is also credited with being a founder of the Tea Party movement, and the organizer of the first Tea Party event.[8]

His resume reportedly includes "work as CEO of MCSNet, a Chicago networking and Internet company; time with D&D Software/ Macro Computer Solutions; work as a programming team leader for network software; and service in network engineering with ratings as a Unix System administrator." [9]

Mr. Denninger was "out of the gate" early, with a video posted the same day as Obama's birth certificate release, claiming that it was all a scam. His videos on the Obama birth certificate have been viewed more than 300,000 times.[10]

Douglas B. Vogt

Douglas Vogt is the owner of Archive Index Systems in Bellevue, Washington. He's the author of an affidavit filed in the Louisiana court case of *Hornbeck v. Salazar*. In that affidavit, Mr. Vogt claims, based on six separate points, that Mr. Obama's birth certificate is a forgery.[11]

Mr. Vogt followed up the original six-page affidavit with an expanded twenty-two-page document which, according to *WorldNetDaily*, has been filed as a complaint with the FBI.[12] Vogt doesn't pull any punches in his analysis, stating:

"I have irrefutably proven that the Certificate of Live Birth that President Obama presented to the world on April 27, 2011 is a fraudulently created document put together using the Adobe Photoshop or Illustrator programs and the creation of this forgery... constitutes a class B felony in Hawaii and multiple violations under U.S. Code... and [is] therefore an impeachable offense."

"When this comes to the public's attention, it will be the greatest scandal in the country's history – nothing comes even close. This will surpass all previous scandals including the Watergate scandal of the Nixon administration."

Mr. Vogt states that he owned a typesetting company for 11 years, as well as a scanner business for 19 years, and that he is well familiar with document imaging systems and software.[13] Dr. Jerome Corsi has described Douglas Vogt as "an international expert on scanners and document imaging software," [14] and as "one of the top experts in the world on scanners." [15]

Douglas Vogt's overall conclusion (which he repeats in a 28-page *Final Analysis*) is that the birth certificate is an "outrageous and obvious" fraud. In this final document, he calls for Congressional hearings and for the FBI to investigate the commission of multiple felonies.[16]

Albert Renshaw

The day that Barack Obama's long-form birth certificate was released, a YouTube user with the nickname of orangegold1 posted a video titled, "*Obama Birth Certificate Faked in Adobe Illustrator – Official Proof.*" [17]

Orangegold1's real name is Albert Renshaw, and although he lists his age in his YouTube profile as 37, it's clear from his web site, *AlbertRenshaw.com*, that his actual age is at least 20 years younger.[18]

Just because Albert is young, however, doesn't mean that his theory is necessarily wrong. Many others far older have looked at the document and concluded the same thing. Albert Renshaw was simply one of the first to post a video making the claim, having immediately noticed several interesting things about the document.

Albert followed up his initial video with three more, answering objections from skeptics. At the time I write this, Albert

Renshaw's YouTube videos have so far generated roughly 1.3 million views – and counting.

Alex Jones

Alex Jones is a talk radio host based in Austin, Texas. According to *Wikipedia*, his syndicated radio program is broadcast on more than 60 radio stations across the United States. He also runs the web site *infowars.com*.[19]

Mr. Jones is not a computer expert, but he is a media personality and has been important in spreading the reports of fraud. His YouTube videos dealing with the possibility of forgery in Obama's birth certificate have generated roughly 1 million views.[20] His broadcast radio shows have reached an unknown number more.

Ivan Zatkovich

Ivan Zatkovich works as an expert witness in court cases, and has 28 years of experience in the computer field. He is the main consultant of *eCompConsultants*.[21]

Mr. Zatkovich was hired by *WorldNetDaily* to produce an expert report on Mr. Obama's birth certificate. The report that he produced runs 16 pages.[22]

Dr. Neal Krawetz

Neal Krawetz, founder of Hacker Factor Solutions (with a web site at *hackerfactor.com*), is a well known specialist in computer forensics and security. He is the author of three books and numerous articles. He holds a PhD in Computer Science from Texas A&M University.[23]

Dr. Krawetz, an expert in the inner workings of graphics files, commented on the birth certificate shortly after its release, stating, "I see nothing that appears to be suspicious." [24]

Nathan Goulding

Nathan Goulding is Chief Technology Officer for *National Review*, a major conservative magazine founded in 1955, and described as "America's most widely read and influential magazine and web site for conservative news, commentary, and opinion." [25]

Mr. Goulding's major contribution has been an early article in which he dismissed the layers-fraud theory. He stated that the layers seen in the White House PDF are a normal feature of these kinds of files, and that he had easily duplicated the phenomenon. [26]

Kevin Davidson

Kevin Davidson, known on the web as "Dr. Conspiracy," retired in January 2011 from 30 years in commercial software development. This included work with scanning and imaging systems for state vital records systems in nine states. [27]

Mr. Davidson is the proprietor of *obamaconspiracy.org*, an information-packed blog dealing with Obama conspiracy theories. He describes the blog's point of view as skeptical of such theories, stating, "Whenever a claim is made that is improbable or spectacular, evidence is expected before the claim is accepted."

Davidson states that he voted for Barack Obama in the 2008 election. [28]

Paul Irey

Paul Irey, according to *WorldNetDaily*, is a retired professional typographer with 50 years experience in the business.

Irey states, "My analysis proves beyond a doubt that it would be impossible for the different letters that appear in the Obama birth certificate to have been typed by one typewriter." [29] He therefore concludes that the document is a forgery.

These seem to be the most prominent and important people in the forgery debate. In this book I will closely and carefully examine their major theories, to see which hold water and which don't.

At least three other individuals have also been named as experts in articles by *WorldNetDaily:* authors Gary Poyssick[30] and Mara Zebest,[31] and software designer Tom Harrison.[32]

Since I noted nothing that was different from other sources in either Gary Poyssick's comments or Ms. Zebest's 12-page report, we will not need to cover these two individuals specifically. We will, however, look at Mr. Harrison's work.

By the end of this book, we will discover good reason to disagree with a number of those on our list of experts.

THE WHITE HOUSE
OFFICIAL PDF

Three Competing Theories

There are three major theories that we might use to explain the oddities observed in the official birth certificate PDF file.

The first theory – the one that set the Internet on fire – is that the file was fraudulently assembled by a human being, using Adobe Photoshop or a similar program.

We can call this the *Graphic Artist* theory. This is the main theory put forth by people who claim the document is forged. However, it's not the only possible forgery theory, as we shall see.

A second theory is that all of the unusual effects we see in the birth certificate PDF were created by computer software acting on a scanned image – with very little in the way of specific human intervention.

This allows for the fact that a human being may have given one or more commands to a computer program to change the image in some way. But by this theory, any such commands were just general commands, and they *weren't* for the purpose of fraud.

A good example of this kind of process is Optical Character Recognition, or OCR.

In OCR, the computer, at the urging of a human being, runs a software program against an image. The software then carefully examines the image to see whether it can detect written characters, whether letters or numbers. And wherever it can detect one or the other, the software does its best to identify it.

OCR, then, is basically a process where the computer tries to read an image and convert any *pictures* of text into *actual* text – of the same kind that you or I would type into the computer. You can then copy the detected text into a word processing document, and edit it... which you usually *want* to do, because computers (as we'll see later) most often do a less-than-perfect job of converting the detected text.

If you're a real glutton for punishment, you can even have the computer read your converted text out loud to you, in a tinny and annoying computer voice. I personally advise against it, as the technology isn't advanced enough yet. But it can be done.

We'll talk more about Optical Character Recognition later.

We can call our second theory, the theory that the image was modified by computer software for (most likely) innocent purposes, the *Software Processing* theory.

Those are the two major theories, but they needn't be mutually exclusive. What if *both* things happened? That's a possibility, too.

Our third theory, then, is that *some* of the things we see are the results of harmless computer processing, but that somewhere along the way, a human being edited the document – with an intent to deceive.

We'll call our third theory the *Processed and Edited* theory.

And we will see which of our three theories better fits the facts.

Let's begin by examining the feature of the PDF file that first launched the cries of "Fraud!"

Does the Existence of "Layers" Prove a Fraud?

"It's a joke-level fraud."[33]

– *Dr. Jerome Corsi, Interview With Alex Jones*

Almost immediately after the long-form birth certificate file was released by the White House, somebody downloaded it and noticed that it contained "layers" of graphic information. These "layers" consist of eight separate graphic images that basically float on top of a mostly-green background.

What Layers Are All About

Anyone who does any serious graphics editing on a computer knows that the standard approach for working with graphics involves the use of *layers*.

Graphic layers have been around for a long time, and there are a lot of people who use them. I personally have worked with layers in computer graphics programs for more than 11 years.

Being able to "layer" things over each other gives a great deal of flexibility and power. It lets you move elements of your graphic around independently. If you decide you need to change something, you can do so without having to rework the entire image. Instead, you simply change the *one* element that you want to change, and everything else is unbothered.

As a simple example of how this works, let's suppose that you decide to make a Christmas card. You begin with a digital photo of your family or yourself, and you put the text "Merry Christmas!" in the upper left corner.

With the old-style, non-layered approach, you use a very simple graphic editing program to add the text to the photo, and you permanently change the photo graphic itself in the process.

In February, you decide you want to use the same image for a "Happy Valentine's Day" card. Unfortunately, even if you can get rid of the "Merry Christmas!" text, you've already messed up all those parts of the picture that were *behind* your message. And there's not really any way to get them back.

You can draw something in their place, but that won't get you quite the same result. More importantly, it takes more of your time and effort. So your best approach is probably to go hunt for the original photo, and start all over.

All of this is avoided when you use *layers*. With layers, you simply make your "Merry Christmas" message an editable layer of text that "floats" as if it's lying on top of the photo. The entire original photo *under* the text is also kept intact – stored separately inside the graphic file.

If you want to move the "Merry Christmas" message to some different corner of the photo later, you can. As soon as you move the text, you see the parts of the picture that were previously hidden behind it. And if you want to edit your message and make it read "Happy Hanukah" or "Happy Valentine's Day," it's a snap.

You can also add additional layers to your picture. You might want five or six of them. You can put layers on top that only contain a heart, or one of Santa's elves. At Christmastime, you could "turn on" the Santa's elf layer to make it visible, and "turn off" the heart layer, to make it invisible, and then print the image without it.

In February, you could make the elf disappear and the heart show up again – all without messing up anything else in your image.

It's little wonder that the theory of fraud immediately caught fire, because a lot of people understand what layers are commonly used for. It's much less common knowledge that graphic editing by a human being is not the *only* process that can produce such a "layered" effect in a computer graphics file.

When people interact directly with layers, it's for a reason: *graphic editing.* So the obvious theory was that Obama's birth certificate file had been created, or at least had been edited, using a graphic editor such as the famous Photoshop.

One Good Reason Why Layers Don't Mean Fraud

It turns out that there are many reasons why this theory – that the layers prove fraud – falls apart. In my YouTube videos, I listed about a *dozen* reasons. But some of those were not conclusive. And in fact, we really need only *one* good one. And we have it.

To understand that reason, we need to think for a moment about low-quality and high-quality images.

It's very easy, graphically speaking, to get from a nice, crisp, clean, sharp photo to a really blurry one. All you have to do is run some sort of graphic effect that blurs the image.

On the other hand, it's generally not possible to start with a really blurry image and produce from it a very crisp image that shows a lot of details you could never see in the original blurred image.

Why not? It's because your original (blurred) image simply didn't contain those details.

Now it's true that you can "sharpen" images or otherwise enhance them graphically – but that capability is limited. All it does, really, is pull out and bring to the forefront information that is there but only very subtly presented.

Later in this book, we will see how limited such graphic enhancement is. You can't recreate genuine details that just were not in the photo to start with.

And this applies not only to blurriness, but also to general quality. With very limited exception, you just can't get from a really low-quality image to a high-quality one.

If the long-form PDF file from the White House is the *original, hand-created computer graphics file*, then, there should not exist a much more detailed image of Obama's birth certificate than that file.

Let's think about that.

If a separate, cleaner and clearly more *detailed* image does exist, then there would've been *no reason* to try to duplicate that by hand-creating a fraudulent PDF – and every reason *not* to... unless of course, there were substantial (fraudulent) changes between the more detailed image and the edited PDF. And in that case, the forger who made those changes would want to *hide* the more detailed original at all costs.

And if someone started out by making a low-quality forgery (which makes little sense in itself), but later decided that they needed a high-quality job, they wouldn't at that point make the low-quality forgery the official file they release to the public.

They would hide or destroy the low-quality forgery, and only release the high-quality one.[34]

Why? To do otherwise would be to recklessly risk detection, because now you have two independent forgeries out there, and they're bound to differ in some subtle way.

So if a much higher-quality image exists, then we have a problem with the *Graphic Artist* theory.

But in fact, we *do* have a much more detailed, higher-quality image of Obama's certificate than the one in the PDF file.

A "white-background" image was released by the Associated Press on April 27, the very same day as the official PDF.[35]

White House Official PDF

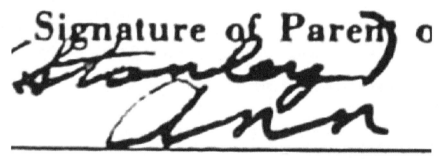

Associated Press Image
(note, for example, clarity of i, g, a's, e's)

2 - The AP Image Shows More Detail than the Official PDF

Note that there exist some significant differences between this document and the official long-form PDF.

First, the AP document does not seem to have a green safety paper background. It appears to have a plain white background instead.

That's odd. Our investigations, however, will lead us to discover *why* that is.

Secondly, the AP document contains faintly visible shadows of *something* behind it. These faint shadows can be enhanced to improve the contrast and make the background image more visible:

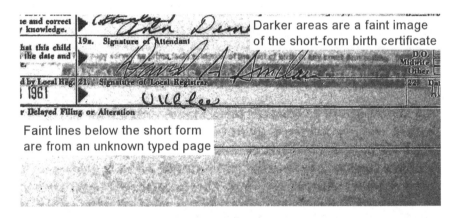

3 - Enhanced View of a Portion of the AP "White-Background" Document

When we enhance the image, we find that there are not one, but two documents behind this one.

Upon close examination, the first document proves to be a copy of the Obama short-form birth certificate. The second document, only part of which is visible below the short-form birth certificate, is a printed sheet of paper of some kind.

There's an important conclusion that we might draw: *the white-background image was most likely a scan of some kind, done from a real piece of paper.*

This conclusion isn't certain at this point, but it seems very likely.

The third difference, of course, is that this document contains details that are clearly of higher graphic quality than the White House PDF. Compare any of the individual characters in Illustration 2, and you will see that this is the case.

Why a Mysterious White-Background Image?

The existence of this image at first seemed a bit of a mystery to me. It wasn't quite clear why the White House would release a white-background copy of the birth certificate.

I first assumed (mistakenly, as it turns out) that the Hawaii Department of Health had released not only a standard, certified copy of the birth certificate, but also a plain paper copy, perhaps for clarity's sake in making a copy to show to the public.

It became clear from "overlaying" the two documents, one on top of the other (and resizing as needed), that they were *identical* in content, showing only a small "warp" effect that is not at all unusual, and is easily explained by there having been, at some point, two separate scans.

This was where my mistaken assumption began to fall apart.

At first, I had completely missed the significance of two items on the AP document that turn out to be rather important. Then one evening, I suddenly noticed what I had been missing:

The "white background" AP document contains the same date and registrar stamps as the green-background PDF file – *and in the exact same places.*

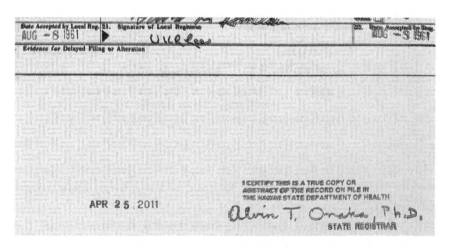

4 – Overlay: The AP and PDF Date and Registrar Stamps Are in the Same Place

This meant that my assumption had major problems. A plain paper copy provided by the Department of Health should *not* have date and registrar certification stamps – and if it did, they wouldn't be in the exact same places as on the green certificate. The odds of that happening by chance were... impossible.

Could it be that the Hawaii Department of Health had first stamped a document, and then made photocopies of it, placing one of those on plain paper and copying another onto green safety paper in order to create the *official* copy?

This too made no sense whatsoever. They wouldn't use a photocopy of an official stamp on a certified document. They would use a *real* stamp.

Clearly, I was missing or misunderstanding something here.

And then I saw something else.

Faint Marks Provide A Critical Clue

In the shaded area on the left side of the AP document, there are faintly visible marks of what looks like a safety paper background.

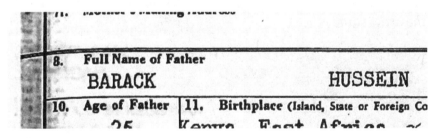

5 – A Faint Safety-Paper Background Is Visible At the Left of the AP Image

Had the original document been on a safety paper background *before* being photographed or scanned at the Hawaii Department of Health?

When I overlaid the white-background document and the green-background PDF image, the truth began to emerge: the safety paper marks on the white-background AP document coincide exactly with the similar marks on the green safety-paper PDF image.

But were these marks *from that same safety paper* – meaning that the white-background document was an image of a green-safety-paper one) – or were they marks from some *earlier* safety paper that was photographically reproduced on *both* documents... *in addition to* the green safety-paper background on the PDF?

The way to determine this for sure was to "project" from the safety paper marks on the non-shaded area of the PDF, using those existing marks to find out exactly *where* the pattern of similar marks ought to appear in the shaded area.

When I did this, the truth became clear: the marks in the shaded area, on *both* documents, *are exactly where we would expect them to be if they are part of the green safety paper background which is seen throughout the official PDF image.*

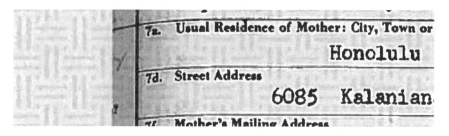

6 – The Safety Paper Pattern is Continuous – Inside of the Shadow and Out

A Breakthrough in Our Understanding

This leads to an inescapable conclusion: The marks in the shaded area of the white-background document *come from the exact same safety-paper background that we see in the green-background document.* Therefore, both of these documents have a common origin. They come from the same place.

In fact, *they are images of the exact same document, and the exact same safety paper background.*

So why doesn't the safety-paper background show up in most of the Associated Press document? Why is it only in the shaded area?

It's because the process that was used to duplicate the image was one that only picked it up at the places where it was at its darkest – and *that* was only in the shaded area at the left.

This rather strongly suggests that the AP image might be a *photocopy* – because photocopies often aren't very good at picking up subtle details like a safety-paper background.

Two New Images Emerge

A skeptic at this point may ask, "Okay. The two documents have to be images of the same thing. That does seem clear."

"But perhaps they both come from a *computer file* that was hand-created in Photoshop. Is the background that we see actual, *real* safety paper, from a genuine paper document, or is it just an *image* of safety paper?"

While I was chewing on the realization that our first two images come from the same place, a new bit of info came along.

Two files had been posted online by Savannah Guthrie, the White House correspondent for NBC News. Both of them claimed to show the Obama birth certificate.

Ms. Guthrie had stated, in MSNBC's report, "I was actually given an opportunity to look at this birth certificate today. I felt the raised seal, I saw the names, the date, the place of birth."

And online, on the same page with one of her images, she posted: "I saw the certified copy of long-form POTUS birth certificate today, felt the raised seal, snapped this pic." [36]

So now we had two online images to back up Savannah Guthrie's claims (or not, as the case might be.)

They needed to be tested.

Now her higher-resolution image is of better quality than the PDF image. The lower-resolution one is, well, low-resolution. But it will still prove useful to us.

A graphic overlay of the Guthrie image with the white-background AP one confirms that, aside from some difference in quality and a little bit of distortion (which, again, is typical when looking at two independent images of the same document), the two are identical.

7 - Graphic Overlay of the White-Background AP Document and Guthrie Photo

But are we certain that the entire thing is the same? Maybe only the birth certificate part is identical, and not the certifying stamps.

Guthrie's shot of the full document is very low resolution, but a second overlay, placing this with the AP document, shows that (again, considering a very small amount of distortion) the date and registrar stamps appear right in the same positions.

of Mother: City, Town or Rural Location	7b. Island	7c. County and State or Foreign Cou
Honolulu	Oahu	Honolulu, Hawaii

6085 Kalanianaole Highway	7e. Is Residence Inside City or Town Limits? If no, give judicial district Yes ☒ No ☐

Address	7g. Is Residence on a Farm or Plan Yes ☐ No ☒

ther		9. Race of Father
HUSSEIN	OBAMA	African

11. Birthplace (Island, State or Foreign Country)	12a. Usual Occupation	12b. Kind of Business or Industry
Kenya, East Africa	Student	University

me of Mother		14. Race of Mother
ANN	DUNHAM	Caucasian

16. Birthplace (Island, State or Foreign Country)	17a. Type of Occupation Outside Home During Pregnancy	17b. Date Last V
Wichita, Kansas	None	

ove stated nd correct owledge.	18a. Signature of Parent or Other Informant	Parent ☒ Other ☐	18b. Date of Sig 8-7-61
this child date and	19a. Signature of Attendant	M.D. ☒ D.O. Midwife Other	19b. Date of Si 8-8-61
Local Reg. 51	21. Signature of Local Registrar		22. Date Accepted by Reg. AUG -8 1961
dlayed Filing or Alteration			

I CERTIFY THIS IS A TRUE COPY OR
ABSTRACT OF THE RECORD ON FILE IN
THE HAWAII STATE DEPARTMENT OF HEALTH

APR 25 2011

Alvin T. Onaka, Ph.D,
STATE REGISTRAR

8 – Overlay: The Stamps Are Also in the Same Places in AP and Guthrie Images

We must therefore conclude that the AP and Guthrie files are *also* different pictures of the same original document. This will soon lead us to an important conclusion.

Scanned Images, Photographs, or Artwork?

As Karl Denninger has noted, a scanner tends to produce some variations in color on the opposite sides of items in the scan. This is called "chromatic aberration."

Since "chromatic" means color, and "aberration" means change, the phrase simply means "*changes in color.*" Cameras can also produce "chromatic aberration" as well.

The AP document shows clear signs of this effect. The top and right edges of the letters have a bluish tint, and the bottom and left edges have a pink one:

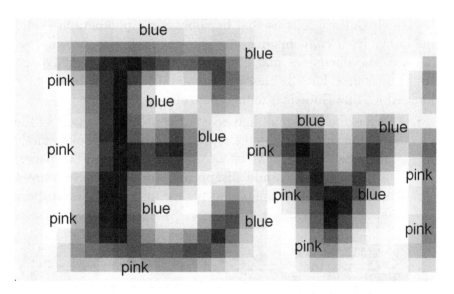

9 - The "White-Background" AP Document Shows Changes in Color

It is therefore a photograph or a scan – even if it originally started out, before being printed, as artwork done in Photoshop.

We can therefore refine our theory regarding the AP document. It appears that an "original" document (whatever that may mean) may have been photocopied, and then that photocopy was either scanned into a computer, or photographed.[37]

In fact, a bit of extra research finds numerous news sites that describe the white-background image as "a *handout* image provided by the White House" – confirming this theory.[38]

Perhaps I should've spent more time reading the Associated Press, and less time staring at the document.

Ah, well. No matter. The fact is, we would've wanted to test it anyway, to confirm what they were telling us. And our having arrived at the conclusion for ourselves, without their help, only makes the point a bit stronger.

Is Guthrie's Image a Photograph, as She Claims?

Savannah Guthrie tells us that her image is a photograph – and the image itself confirms this. Aside from an obvious brown desk beneath the document and a stack of papers to the left (which could of course have been Photoshopped), we have three *other* indications that Guthrie is telling the truth:

1.   We can see a small lighter-colored area in the part of the photograph that has the registrar's seal. This looks exactly like the play of light off of a slight crinkle in the paper. Such a crinkle would disappear if the document were a scan, because scanners and photocopiers flatten out these kinds of things.

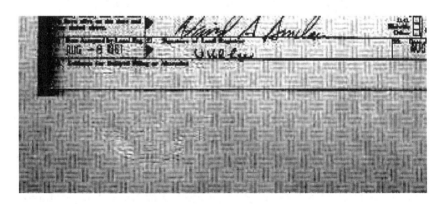

10 – A Lighter-Colored "Crinkle" is Visible at Bottom Left of the Seal

2. The image has *perspective*. The perspective is visible, and when we measure it, we find that the image is about 1.5% narrower at the top than at the bottom.

    In addition, the edge lines of the paper are very slightly *curved*. If perspective had been added artificially using a graphics program, any such lines would probably be straight rather than curved.

    The perspective indicates that this image was likely taken with a camera. In fact, the image seems to have been photographed from exactly the kind of angle you would normally expect.

3. Finally, there is a subtle shift in color towards the bottom right of the image. This becomes more evident with a bit of graphic enhancement. If the document were a scan, then the entire background would be one single color.

We therefore do not have to simply take Savannah Guthrie's word when she tells us that she saw and handled a paper document and felt its seal.

We can safely conclude, on the basis of all the evidence from the documents as well, that Savannah Guthrie's image is a photo – just as she claims.

A photo of a *real and physical paper document*.

Multiple Identical Documents, or Just One?

We've established the fact that safety paper markings appear in the shaded area in the same places on the AP and PDF documents, and that these markings are in exactly the right places to be part of the green safety paper background.

Overlaying the Guthrie and PDF images confirms that the safety-paper markings appear in the exact same places on the Guthrie photograph as well.

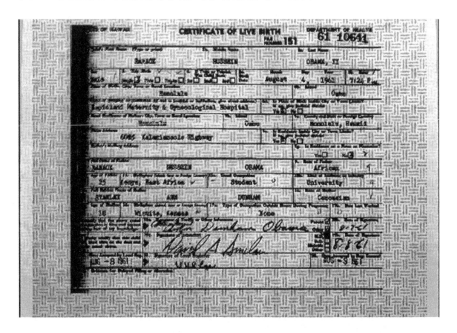

11 – Overlay: Safety-Paper Markings Are Identical in Guthrie & PDF Images

It's only possible for this to be the case if all three are images of the same document, *or* of identical documents in which the safety-paper designs are perfectly aligned (which also means they would have to have come from the same office, and would most likely have been printed at the same time).

Of the two possibilities, it seems more likely that they are images of the exact same physical paper document, because we wouldn't really expect two sheets of safety paper to match exactly. But – we can further confirm that theory.

We've also established, critically, that the *date and registrar certification stamps* appear in the same places on all three documents.

And *this* is only possible if the images are of the same physical document, or if they are images of documents so identical that they have their stamps *in the exact same locations.*

And the latter, practically speaking, could only happen if someone constructed identical documents by reproducing the entire document, with the date and registrar stamps *already on them*. (But in a moment, we will find that we can eliminate that case.)

Three Images Converge

The State of Hawaii issued a press release the same day as the birth certificate release, stating clearly that they had provided two certified copies of Barack Obama's long-form birth certificate.

However, nowhere do government offices produce certified copies of documents by duplicating documents that already have their official stamps.

The practice, if multiple copies are needed, is *always* to stamp and seal the different copies individually, using actual office stamps on each.

For them to deviate from this practice in this case, aside from most likely being illegal, would only cause needless questions of authenticity.

By any reasonable standard of proof, then, we may consider the following conclusion to be inescapable:

All three of these images are images of the same physical paper document – the paper document of which Savannah Guthrie said, "I felt the raised seal, I saw the names, the date, the place of birth." [39]

This conclusion, while inescapable, is utterly at odds with what many people perceive about the PDF image of the document.

Given that the PDF image (however altered graphically) undeniably shows the exact same *physical, paper* document, with the exact same *information* as both the AP image and Savannah Guthrie's two photographs, it *cannot* have been fraudulently edited in the layers we see in the PDF file.

This means that not only is our *Graphic Artist* theory false – so too is our *Processed and Edited* theory. We have very neatly killed two of our three theories with one stone.

On first reading, this may not be quite obvious – but if you retrace our steps and think back through it carefully, I believe the conclusion is *inescapable*.

If the PDF document is identical, except for such things as layers and image quality and internal oddities, *to a known and photographed physical document* on green safety paper, then it quite simply *was not* edited in such a way as to change any information after the paper document was scanned.

So why the layers? Why the other things we observe?

Only one of our three possible theories remains as an explanation for all of the oddities: The *Software Processing* theory, which claims that the features we see in the PDF were caused by the more-or-less automatic operation of computer software.

Now if the *Software Processing* theory can be disproven by anything that we see in the PDF file, we will end up with a major contradiction of reality on our hands.

Our next order of business, then, is to closely examine the official PDF.

WHERE THE LAYERS CAME FROM

"If they scanned this, which they say they did,
it would all be on one layer." [40]

– Albert Renshaw, YouTube Video

So what are we to do with the fact of the layers?

In this chapter we will see if we can determine whether these were the result of a mostly computer process, or a mostly human one. We will also aim to unravel what *kind* of process it was – and by that, I mean its *purpose.*

By the way, someone who knows Adobe Illustrator is likely to complain about my use of the term "layers." They will insist that there is only *one* layer in the document. And strictly speaking, this is true. This one layer contains nine different *elements,* or bits of content.

However, since these elements can be overlaid on top of each other, they behave in much the same way as "layers" might in some other graphics programs.

And since the term "layers" has been so widely used to describe these independent elements, I will continue using that word for the purposes of this book.

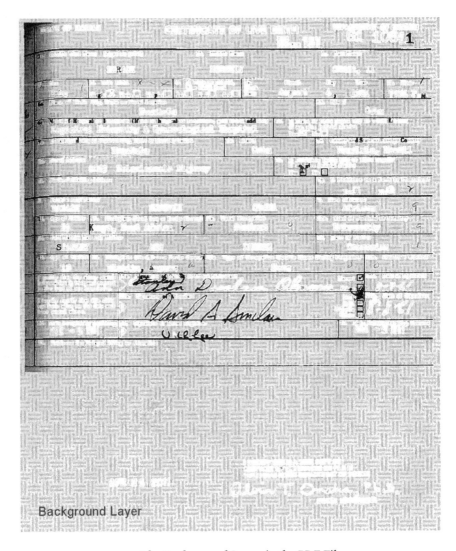

Background Layer

12 - The Background Layer in the PDF File

We can immediately note some things about these layers, images of which I show here.

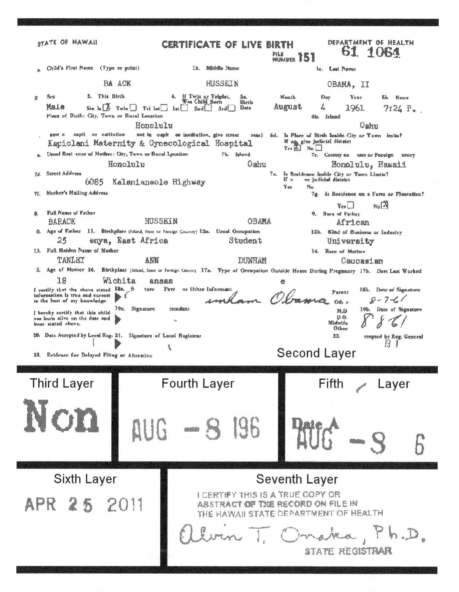

13 - The Most Important Remaining Layers in the PDF File

By the way, since two of our layers only look like a bit of white-colored "noise," I've left those two out. The illustrations include those layers that show the background and obvious content.

Layers, But Not as We Know Them

The first thing we ought to observe is that all but the last two of these layers would be very strange from the standpoint of a human being creating or editing a document.

When a human being creates a graphic document, the normal practice (as we noted in the example of your Christmas card) is to use editable text layers. That's *not* what we have here. All we have here are *images* or *pictures* of text.

Unlike your "Merry Christmas," these aren't editable at all – except in the same way that you might *graphically* edit a photo.

Secondly, bits and pieces of what you and I would naturally identify as being parts of the same thing are split out into completely different layers or elements.

For example, Stanley Ann Obama's signature is split across two layers. Part of it is solid black, and part of it is grayscaled (and by this, we mean presented in various shades of gray). Bits and pieces of the date stamps are on different layers, too.

Let's go item by item and point out what's strange.

First, a background layer normally contains just that: a background. But here, we have a lot more than just the safety-paper background. *That* has been messily altered by a bunch of things that are now permanently embedded in it.

Those things include:

- the lines of the form.
- with very few exceptions, *only* those letters of the form which touch the lines, or which touch something *else* that touches a line. And the very few exceptions to this rule are arguably close enough that some "bleed" runs into the line.
- about half of the check boxes (again, *only* those that touch the lines of the form).
- the "1" of the birth certificate number.
- seven, and *only* seven, of the typed characters.
- those parts of the signatures that touch the form lines.
- and a whitish "shadow" of everything else.

Our second layer contains almost all of the printed and typed lettering of the form.

So the lines of the form are on one layer; but almost all of the *letters* of the form are on another layer... except for "Date A," which appears on a *third* layer.

The actual form itself is therefore spread out over *three* layers.

Now there are only two ways to get the image of a government form into something like Photoshop. You either have to scan it in, or you have to draw it. Drawing it would be far more laborious – taking probably *days* worth of effort.

And unless you were *extremely* careful, it would be very much subject to mistakes that could give away your entire forgery.

Now in either case, something like a form would normally start out in a single layer, and *stay* in that single layer.

But here, about half of the check boxes and all three of the triangle-shaped "arrows" from the form are on the second layer.

The form, in short, is a complete mess.

The Mess Continues

The third layer consists of *only* the "Non" from the typewritten word "None."

The fourth layer contains all of the local registrar date stamp... *except for* the final "1" in "1961."

The fifth layer consists of the Registrar General date stamp (except for the "1," "9," and "1" in "1961"), the letters from the form that touch the date stamp, and (oddly) one of the dashes from the handwritten date above it. All the rest of the handwritten date has been left behind back on layer two.

If someone created this document using Photoshop or some similar program, it would appear that they did a very careless job.

Except that "careless" really isn't a possibility.

When working in a graphics program, even carelessly, you *don't* get things spread over different layers at random like this. *In order for a human being to put these things on different layers, they would have to have been placed on their specific layers quite deliberately, every single separate item one at a time.*

In other words, someone would have had to make the *decision* to first draw the lines of the form, and then add all of the letters that touch those lines.

Then they would have had to decide to *split up* the date stamps between two layers.

If they were scanning in a real item, such as an actual form, they would then have had to go and manually separate out all of the things that we see separately, such as all of the form letters, and then quite deliberately move them to different layers.

All of this would be both an utter waste of time and a needless risk for getting caught – if you're a human being trying to forge a document.

The Other Possibility

All of this, however, is reasonable if you happen to be a computer program just trying (rather ineptly in comparison to human capability) to make sense of a scanned image – and then splitting things into different layers for some computer purpose.

But what purpose? To me, as someone who works with graphic files, two possible and very useful purposes immediately became evident.

The first of these is Optical Character Recognition (OCR).

Optical Character Recognition (as we noted earlier) happens when a computer program looks at a scanned image and tries to read it and convert it to text.

And the expected result of Optical Character Recognition is actual *characters of text* – just like the ones you typed into your Christmas card photo.

Since there are *no* actual characters of text at all in the PDF file – only *pictures* of text – we can safely conclude that Optical Character Recognition was *not* a factor here.

The second possible purpose is what is called "optimization."

Why Graphic Files Are "Optimized"

Several years ago, digital photography became popular – along with uploading one's photos to the computer. At the time, a lot of people were still on a dial-up Internet connection.

The result of this unhappy combination was often disastrous. People would upload their photos to the computer, and then try to e-mail them to their friends (some of whom were not their friends for very long afterward, I'm afraid.)

The problem was that the digital photos created files that were way too big to be handled easily by a slow dial-up Internet connection. Lots of people who had dial-up Internet found themselves waiting an hour or more just to collect their e-mail! Their in-boxes – and their entire Internet connections – had been clogged with enormous graphic files.

It was kind of like bringing an elephant in through the hallway. Nothing could get past it, and you couldn't go anywhere or do anything until you had gotten the elephant unclogged.

This problem has mostly been solved since then, for two reasons. One is that a lot more people have high-speed Internet connections. But also, most who work with digital photographs have learned to optimize their images.

Optimizing is a process in which you run a program on a graphic file that reduces its size, but still leaves the picture with high enough quality to be looked at and enjoyed by a human being.

Different methods, and different programs, are used to optimize files for size and quality.

Our "Software Processing" Theory Becomes the "Software Optimization" Theory

When we look at the size of the PDF file that contains Obama's birth certificate, we find that it is 377 K bytes in size. This is not a bad size for downloading over the Internet. In fact, it's similar in size to a standard, optimized JPG (or "JPEG," pronounced "jay-peg") picture file.[41]

This 377 KB represents the *equivalent* of about 7.6 million pixels of information.

Now when you scan an image of this size using a scanner – *without* doing optimization of some kind – you get a file that is much larger than this.

In comparison, one version of the Associated Press JPEG graphic (downloaded from *delawarenow.com*) uses around 920 KB to represent approximately 3.3 million pixels. Strictly speaking, it isn't a higher *resolution* image, because it represents fewer pixels. But it's a higher *quality* image, because its pixels represent the image more accurately.

This AP image file produces its higher quality at a cost of spending, on the average, about 5.6 times as much storage space *per pixel* as the White House PDF.

We have actual proof, then, in the file size itself, *that the White House file has been optimized in some way.* This is not unusual; in fact, it's normal to optimize images posted on the web.

Perhaps the layers were created, extracted from the original single scanned layer, as part of this optimization.

We have a theory, then, for *why* a computer program might create these layers. But it would certainly help if we had an example of a computer file that was scanned and optimized in a very similar way.

It turns out that we do.

In fact, we have more than one.

Documents That Have Layers

First, Nathan Goulding of *National Review* was able to substantially duplicate the layers effect, on the very day that Obama's PDF file was released. His demonstration was promptly posted on the *National Review* web site.[42]

Now when I first attempted to duplicate the effects seen in the Obama PDF (including the specific *kind* of layers it has), I must confess that I ran into a few snags.

For example, it was really easy to find PDF documents that divided into layers when opened with Adobe Illustrator... but in most cases, the layers were simple slices of the entire document.

The top one-fourth of the document, sliced horizontally, might be the first layer, with the second fourth of the document being the second layer, and so on.

This isn't how the Obama PDF is divided up.

Well, as Neal Krawetz, one of our commentators on the Obama PDF, noted, there are many, *many* ways to put together a PDF file.[43]

And there are even *more* ways to optimize one.

In fact, when I started calculating the different combinations of settings to optimize a PDF, I quickly learned that there weren't just hundreds of ways to do it, or even thousands.

With all of the many possible options, the possibilities quickly ran into the *billions* – and beyond.

Nonetheless, I now have an almost limitless source of files that duplicate nearly every feature of the Obama PDF file, and do so to a very high degree.

The *only* significant oddity of the Obama PDF that I've still had a bit of difficulty with, using automated processes in standard off-the-shelf software, is the white "shadow" effect in the background layer. And it's not that it's hard to duplicate the basic effect itself – *that* part is easy. The difficulty I have found is in getting the "shadow" as *white* as it appears in the Obama PDF.

That, undoubtedly, is a matter of settings, and most likely of software. As we will talk about later, in addition to Adobe Acrobat there are many, many programs that know how to create a PDF file. And probably most of these will do it just a little bit differently.[44]

We will also see later exactly why the white "shadow" may have arisen.

But aside from our small difficulty in getting things bright enough on the shadow, we seem to have an unlimited supply of files that are very, very similar to the Obama PDF.

So let me give you an example other than the Nathan Goulding/ *National Review* one mentioned above.

Below is an image of a page from *The Child's Wonder Picture Book of Favourite Stories,* downloaded in PDF format from Google Books (*books.google.com*).[45]

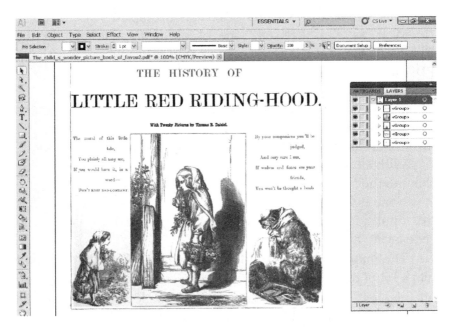

14 – Google Books File Showing Almost All Features of the Obama PDF

The above page is divided into its layers in the following way:
- The middle and left-hand illustrations are one layer.
- The right-hand illustration and a bit of the word "RIDING-HOOD" are a second layer.
- "THE HISTORY OF" is a separate layer.
- And the remaining text is yet another layer.

This is the same type of division into layers we see in the Obama PDF document.

Now it's true that I did have to do something with the original file, but that "something" consisted of only *one* very simple step.

Adobe Illustrator was unable for some reason to open the entire book (too many pages, perhaps?) So in order to produce a PDF that Illustrator could read, I first opened the document in Adobe Acrobat, and then exported only the single page that I wanted.

I did this by "printing" the page to Adobe PDF format.

Then I simply opened the document in Illustrator, with the results mentioned.

How to Duplicate This for Yourself

This is an exercise you can do yourself, if you're so inclined. All you have to do is:

First go to Adobe's web site (*adobe.com*). Download and install trial versions of both *Acrobat* and *Illustrator*. Then, go to *books.google.com*, find an appropriate book (the one I used, or another) and download it in PDF format.

Finally, print a page to PDF from Acrobat, as I did, and open it up in Illustrator.

If you pick the right *kind* of PDF file from Google Books, you ought to be able to see this, and some other relevant effects as well. The files that seem to work best are those from documents new enough to have some consistency in type (don't try books from the 1600's), and old enough *not* to easily run OCR on.

You might try, for example, books dated between 1850 and 1900.

So why do many Google Books show the same layers effect as Obama's PDF? It's because they are optimized before uploading to the web, using similar settings and similar (if not the same) software as that used by the White House.

Why the Weird Optimization?

At this point, it's worth asking, "So why optimize a graphic file in this particular way? What's the advantage?"

The basic reason for such optimization is that human beings (who are the "target audience" that will eventually read the optimized file) deal with visual information in three basic ways.

One of those ways is *text*. People like to read nice, crisp text. If the text is all one solid color, and not a bunch of jumbled up colors or shades, that's a good thing.

But it also needs to be as smooth as possible, otherwise the target audience will be distracted by the jagged edges of the letters. Instead of thinking about the content (which is what you want them to think about), they will think, "This page looks awful. It looks like it was done by a cheap computer."

The second way that people deal with visual information is through solid-color graphics. These include solid areas on a page, as well as "clip art" and line drawings.

15 – Text and Solid-Color Graphics Are Better Represented with Solid Colors

And the third way, of course, is through photographs and works of art that have all kinds of *subtle* colors and shades in them.

The first two kinds of information simply tend to look better when they're presented in solid colors.

And, there's a bit of a "cheat" involved here.

If a program can split out different elements within the image with only a single color, then for that particular element, it only has to store the location of each pixel. It does *not* have to store a separate color value for every one of the pixels involved.

This is a *big* space saver.

Why did I suddenly switch back to using the word "element" instead of the word "layer?" For a very simple reason: The "layers" in the PDF file really *aren't* layers, in the sense that *they don't cover the entire image.*

Instead of layers that would each cover the entire image, what we really have (except, of course, for the background) are smaller, solid-color images that are then placed in various places in the file.

This is obvious when you hover the mouse pointer over each of these in Adobe Illustrator: A blue box surrounds the image and shows you how big it is, and its location.

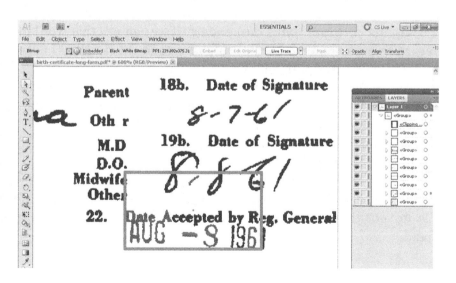

16 – A Blue Box Shows Size and Location of Each Solid-Color Image

Saving space by working with smaller images where possible also explains why the above date stamp and the "Non" in "None," which are the *only* single-color elements that use the exact same single color, are stored as *two* separate images, and not one.

All of the other elements were detected as things that ought to be *different* single colors, which helps explain why we have *those* particular items stored separately.

There's another simple way that the optimizing program saves space, which we'll see later.

Now, not only do we understand the basics of why we have the layers, we've even pretty well solved the mystery of why we have the *specific* layers that we do.

To Sum Up the Layers

We've seen that the kinds of layers found in the Obama PDF make no sense from the point of view of a human being creating a graphic file. For a forger, these would only represent unnecessary extra work, and needless risk of detection.

We've seen that they *do* make sense from the point of view of a computer program trying desperately (if we can use that word in regard to a computer program) to understand the scanned image and optimize it in a particular way.

We've seen that many of the books scanned and optimized by Google Books – and this appears to include *thousands* of them – have very much the same kind of layers as our White House PDF.

And finally, we've seen *why* the optimizing program created the specific layers it did.

We are therefore led to conclude, for the second time, that the layers found in Barack Obama's long-form birth certificate PDF file do *not*, by themselves, mean that the birth certificate is a fraud.

DOES THE TEXT SHOW CLEAR SIGNS OF BEING EDITED?

"The '1' is obviously a picture, a JPEG that was inserted into the document, and the pixels around it show clear evidence of masking. Whoever did this didn't know how to repair the pixels, so the obvious indication is that the JPEG in the place of the number is clearly there. Experts can distinguish these features almost easily." [46]

– Dr. Jerome Corsi, on the Tom Tancredo Show

"The only real part of this signature is the 'Ann D.' Everything else, including the 'Obama,' is faked, and it's obviously faked... Somewhere out there, there is a real birth certificate with a signature, 'Ann D...' This is clearly a fake. There's no doubt about it, and it's pretty poorly done, too." [47]

– Albert Renshaw, YouTube Video

So far, we've seen that the Associated Press photocopy handout, the green-background PDF file released by the White House, and the photos posted by Savannah Guthrie are *all* images of the same physical paper document – and that the information presented on all three images is identical.

And we've seen that the nature of the layers doesn't work for a human forger, but makes total sense from the point of the view of the computer.

All of the evidence so far, then – *all* of it – is in favor of our *Software Optimization* theory.

If it's true that the text shows clear signs of being edited, however, then that's a problem for our theory.

We've explained *why* the background layer is in full color, and why all of the other layers are single-color layers: the program wanted to economically preserve the single-color areas.

It couldn't do this with the background area, however (since it wasn't single-color but multi-color), so it left that as a standard JPEG graphic image. Incidentally, as we shall see (and in harmony with our theory), it also optimized that layer *as a JPEG*.

The JPEG format doesn't allow for "holes" in an image. So it couldn't simply delete the background areas "behind" the solid-color items that it extracted. For this reason, it did something else with them.

So why do all the lines of the *form* belong to the background layer? Why weren't *they* extracted into one of the separate solid-color layers?

The reason is very simple: The lines were too thin for the program to really be able to tell that they ought to be solid-color instead of normal, multi-color graphics – and they were against the green background.

All of the things attached to these form lines were considered likely to be graphics, as well.

After all, it's not *normal,* in most documents such as letters and books, for the text and the illustrations to touch each other.

So if an item touches something that the program has already decided must be a graphic, then (by very reasonable logic on the part of the program) it must be part of the same graphic.

Therefore, all of its subtle shades of color should be kept, and it shouldn't be pulled out into a separate, sharp, single-color layer.

We have claims of editing from Dr. Jerome Corsi, as well as from several other persons prominently involved in the controversy. The rationale for these accusations is simply that part of the document is grayscaled and part is solid-color.

But *virtually none* of the grayscaled items are things that it would be of the *slightest* benefit to a forger to "edit!"

Does Jerome Corsi really think, for example, that a forger manually edited the "H" and the "al" in "Hospital" (which appears on the birth certificate form itself) – *and left the "ospit" alone?*

17 – Did a Forger Really Edit the "H" and "al" in the Form Word "Hospital"?

Not a single person publicly pushing the claim that the document is "clearly edited" has explained *why* their forger would manually edit the "H" and the "al," and leave the "ospit" alone.

As far as I know, not a single one of them has tried.

And of course, this for a very good reason. They *can't* explain it, because it is *completely and utterly unexplainable.*

Believing the *Graphic Artist* theory, then, has the side effect of requiring you to believe in things that simply have no explanation at all.

The Mystery of the Phantom "1"

It turns out that of more than *two dozen* grayscaled items (see our background layer illustration), there's only *one instance* of grayscaling in the entire PDF that might *possibly* be of benefit to a forger to edit.

This is, of course, the one specific instance that Corsi cites – while completely ignoring *all* of the others.

It's the "1" in the birth certificate number.

So why was this particular item not kept as a solid color?

Corsi's explanation is that it was edited by a human being. On the face of it, that explanation seems reasonable – at least until we start looking at all of the *other* grayscaled items. But is there some other reason this character might be different?

In order to find the likely explanation, we should first note that while it's the only grayscaled item that a forger might actually want to edit, it's *not* the only free-standing grayscaled item on the page.

There are three other such typewritten letters on the page.

First is the "R" in "BARACK," near the top of the page.

When we look at the "R" in the high-quality AP document (in which *everything* is grayscaled), we can see some reason *why* this letter might have been grayscaled, rather than detected as a solid-color item. It's a bit fainter than the letters surrounding it. It was struck a bit more lightly by the typist, and didn't leave quite as much of an impression. And like the form lines, it's also *thin*. And, it's a bit broken.

18 – The "R," Struck Lightly, Is a Bit Fainter and Thin (Enhanced Image)

Fainter, lighter, thinner items in the image generally tend to be grayscaled. The optimizing program doesn't believe that they are important text or solid-color graphic items that need to be pulled out into a separate layer. If they had been, the rationale goes, they would've been darker and thicker.

This is seen, for example, with the hand-written pencil markings in the background layer of the document. All of these are grayscaled, too.

19 – AP View of Some Other Items Grayscaled in the PDF

The other grayscaled letters are the "K" in "Kansas" and the "S" in "Stanley."

Again, with the "K," we have an obvious likely reason. While the "K" is dark at the bottom, it fades going up. The top part is entirely blank. This is evidence that the top part of the typewritten "K" didn't strike the ribbon hard enough to leave an impression on the paper.

Something that fades from black to nothing, our program thinks, probably needs to be grayscaled.

The "S" in "Stanley" is a bit more of a mystery, although we should note two things about it: It's pretty thin, and it's at the beginning of a word.

The "S," the "K" and the "1" all have this in common: they are all on the beginning or end of a word. End characters would appear to be a bit more difficult for the program to judge whether to grayscale or make a solid color.

So other than being on the end, is there a particular reason why the "1" might have been left behind when the rest of the certificate number was extracted into another layer?

Quite possibly so. A close look at the top of the form shows that there's a difference between the "1" and the other characters – and it's a very relevant difference.

20 – *The "1" Is the Only Character with Significant Lighter Areas Inside It*

While there are gaps in the second "1" and the "4" (and these show up when we look at the PDF image), the final "1" contains *no* gaps that actually cut into the letter. Like the others, it's "spotty." But instead of open, white gaps, it contains four lighter-colored (but still not white) areas within the body of the "1."

These four lighter-colored areas are apparently enough to cause the optimizing program to decide that the character should be grayscaled, and not all converted to a single color. It just doesn't look quite like a solid letter to the scanning program.

We therefore have a very plausible explanation for why the "1" is grayscaled, and another piece added to our puzzle.

But Wait – It's the Solid-Color Items that Were Edited Instead...

Albert Renshaw, in one of his videos, makes an *opposite* claim: that the grayscaled portion of Stanley Ann Dunham's signature was the original part, but that a forger drew in the solid-colored portion.[48]

(We should probably make clear in passing that this completely conflicts with Corsi's claim that it's the *grayscaled* items that would seem to be the forged ones.)

Aside from the fact that the *Software Optimization* theory fully explains the grayscaled/ solid-color divide, Albert's theory has several other very serious problems.

The first is that no forger in his right mind would create a signature that was half grayscaled and half solid pixels. I don't care *how* dumb the forger is. Any forger who didn't want to get caught would first hand-write a signature on a piece of paper, and then scan *that* in.

The second problem is that it's virtually impossible (at least not without spending hours and hours at the task) to create a convincing signature by drawing it pixel-by-pixel in a graphics program. If anyone disagrees, let them try it; and let them explain why anyone in their right mind (or anyone not in their right mind, for that matter) would attempt to do it that excruciatingly painful way instead of hand-drawing the signature and spending the 60 seconds or so that it takes to scan it in.

The third serious problem is that photos and scans of genuine Stanley Ann Dunham Obama signatures are available out on the Internet. And this one looks very much like the genuine known ones.

This is impossible by Albert's theory, which is that someone started with a real "Ann D..." off of a real birth certificate, erased the last part of the original name, and added "unham." The fact is, the "Ann D" that we have matches Ms. Dunham Obama's real signatures very well, and so does the rest of the name, too.

And the fourth serious problem, of course, is that we have not one, but *two* higher-quality images of the same document, that show very clearly that the latter part of the signature was *not* created by pixel-by-pixel drawing.

Incidentally, as a side note, editing any solid-color item would also have required editing of the white shadow behind it, in order to be convincing.

Albert Renshaw has done some pretty good analysis for a 16-year-old, and I sincerely compliment him on it.

However, the idea that the PDF shows clear editing, for all of the above reasons, is a bust.

WHY IS THE FORM AREA
SLIGHTLY BLURRED?

"As soon as I come down here to the corner... you can see I've got nice, sharp definition here. And as soon as I go inside this area where this is printed, oops – guess what? That nice sharp definition has been blurred...

Somebody took two images, the safety-paper image here, as a background, and then laid this other document on top of it. This is not a scan. This is assembled from... documents that were put together by computerized means." [49]

– Karl Denninger, YouTube Video

Denninger is correct to note that the safety-paper background looks very slightly different in the form area, particularly at the lower right. The background seems a bit more blurred in the form area, and the white parts seem slightly darker.

And his explanation would seem to be a plausible one: that the difference came from the fact that somebody laid a layer over the background.

Except that just adding a regular, transparent layer to a graphic *won't blur the background.*

My first thought was that the slight difference was probably due to the software optimizing the JPEG background layer.

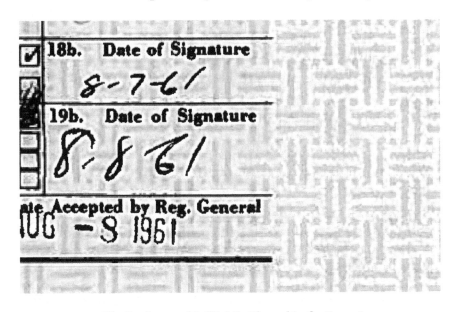

21 – The Background Is Slightly Blurred in the Form Area

JPEG optimization disturbs entire areas of an image, and those disturbances tend to take place in square blocks. Therefore, it seemed very likely to me that optimizing the form area (which includes those dark form lines), would probably blur that entire area just a little bit. (By the way, we can very clearly see that the background layer *was* optimized as a JPEG. This is obvious in the "scattered pixels" right around the darker elements. We'll see an illustration of this in our next chapter.)

However, experiments that I ran on a similar image to test my theory failed to blur the background, even when I tried a few different settings.

Hmmm.

At that point, I came up with a different theory: What I was looking at was probably a tiny bit of gray shadowing from the original document – the very original one that would've been copied onto the safety paper, in order to create the paper certificate that Savannah Guthrie photographed.

However, the photo we have from Savannah Guthrie fails to confirm *this* theory, either. There seems to be no additional shadowing in the form area.

It is at this point, the annoying point at which the author has no real explanation for a particular effect observed, that a great many writers would quietly and discreetly hit the delete button, go for a cup of coffee, and forget about this small chapter – because it fails to provide any visible support for their theory.

But I'm not going to do that. Instead, I'm simply going to note a couple of things:

First, in real life, it's not always possible to identify a brilliant explanation for *every* single point of data observed. This is particularly true when you're dealing with literally dozens of critiques of the item in question. This is not abnormal.

If this is the biggest thing that our theory can't explain (and so far, it is), then we are doing *remarkably* well – and far better than the alternative theories, I might add.

Secondly, this is kind of like live TV. The outcome of this book is not necessarily certain, even to me, even as I write it. If I should discover something new in the process (which I did today while watching one of Denninger's videos that I hadn't yet seen), things could change – right up until the end.

So if you were starting to feel like we were falling into a routine, I hope this will be of comfort to you.

Third, not being able to explain exactly where the feature came from is not a big problem as long as it doesn't provide any compelling evidence that our theory is wrong. And this feature most certainly doesn't.

Yes, it would be *possible* to have such a blurring of the form area as a result of graphic editing, but frankly, it's unlikely.

In order for something to blur the form area, there would have to be some *content* there, perhaps a light gray layer of some sort. And such a layer would *not* just appear on its own. It would have to come from somewhere.

I speak as someone who works with computer graphics.

In other words, Denninger's theory that this blurring is evidence of forgery requires that a forger *deliberately* created a very light-gray layer of some sort in the form area, and/ or deliberately blurred the area. Such things *don't* just magically appear on their own.

But there's no known reason for anyone to do such a thing.

So Denninger's theory is not an explanation at all, any more than our admission is that we don't really know, at this time, quite why the slight difference is there.

Why is it slightly blurred in the form area? I can't really tell you.

Why would a forger have *deliberately created* a slightly blurred area in the form? Denninger can't tell you that, either.

I do have one other possible theory, though. Since this appears *only* in the PDF, perhaps there was some feature or abnormality of the scanner that was used when the document was scanned – or of the scanning *program* – that "bled" the image a bit before it was converted into the PDF, and slightly blurred the form in some spots.

And perhaps that "bleeding" occurred because that entire area of the form, on average, was darker than the areas in which there were *no* black form lines, and no black text.

That might or might not be the right idea; still, it's probably more plausible than Denninger's attributing it to human agency.

In summary, this one is mostly a wash; and as such, it does no harm to our *Software Optimization* theory.

THE MISSING
"CHROMATIC ABERRATION"

"What the Associated Press has here is a scan, and again, there's that chromatic aberration. And guess what's missing here? No chromatic aberration at all. None. Nowhere in this document do I see chromatic aberration, and that's a huge problem... Ladies and gentlemen, this document has been assembled by somebody on a computer." [50]

– Karl Denninger, YouTube Video

We talked earlier about the subtle changes in color that you see around sharp, dark images when you greatly enlarge scans or photographs, and we called this "chromatic aberration."

We also noted that "chromatic aberration" simply means "changes in color."

Karl Denninger claims that there's no chromatic aberration around the black text in the document. Therefore, it can't be a scan, since scanned images have chromatic aberration. This is logical so far.

However, Denninger is perfectly aware of the higher-quality AP document. Oddly, he fails to note the fact that *having* a higher-quality document eliminates any reason whatsoever for anybody to forge the lower-quality PDF.

But I digress.

Denninger states that the PDF document is not a scan, that it was assembled in layers by somebody. And he's almost correct. The only problem is that he assumes that it was assembled by a *person*.

But is he actually right when he claims that there's no chromatic aberration?

As we've seen, most of the letters in this image have been converted to a single color in the optimization process. And "single color" is pretty much the ultimate in "no chromatic aberration."

If there *is* any evidence of chromatic aberration, then, it would have to be present in the *only* layer that consists of more than one color – the background.

It is clear that the background is a JPEG image *that has been graphically optimized.* How do we know this? I simply stated it as a fact a bit earlier, but now we're actually going to see why.

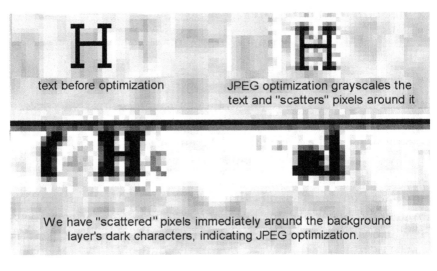

text before optimization

JPEG optimization grayscales the text and "scatters" pixels around it

We have "scattered" pixels immediately around the background layer's dark characters, indicating JPEG optimization.

22 – Scattered Pixels Around Dark Characters Show JPEG Optimization

We can tell it's been optimized because we can easily *see* it. Above is a sample showing what text on a background looks like before and after JPEG optimization, and also showing what our "H...al" (from the word "Hospital") looks like in the Obama PDF.

The "scattered pixels" around the open parenthesis, the capital "H" and the "al" are *exactly* the kind of thing we see around dark text when a JPEG file is optimized.

But in the middle, where the letters "ospit" were, we have a white blur. What are we to do about that?

You may remember that we noted the program can't simply get rid of the pixels "behind" the solid-color letters it extracts for clarity. So it has to do something else with them. Specifically, they have to be given a color value of some sort, even if it's only the color most commonly used for "blank" – which would be *white*.

In most cases, if one wants to avoid creating a real mess, white would, in fact, be the best plain general color to use.

Just to see what will happen, let's run a little experiment. Let's assume – just for the sake of argument – that the optimizing program removed the black pixels into another layer, *and then replaced them with white pixels* before it optimized the background.

Let's try doing something similar, and see what happens.

23 – A Quick Experiment

Now note that we have no idea of the settings used to optimize the Obama PDF background. And there are a couple of different formats used for JPEG images, and we don't know whether we have the right one.

And we *certainly* didn't manage an exact duplication of the document. For one thing, our letters are way too thin.

Nonetheless, what we have, on our very first attempt at such an experiment, looks strikingly similar to what we see in the background layer of the Obama PDF file.

We have our dark letters, now grayscaled (these are the ones that stay in the background, remember), with scattered pixels around them.

And in between, we have a white blur with no obvious scattered pixels, but with some irregularities.

This is *very* much like what we see in the Obama PDF.

Might We Find Any Chromatic Aberration in a Badly Altered Background?

Denninger is quite right that no chromatic aberration is visible.

But then, it *wouldn't* be. Not in a background that has been obviously and profoundly altered by a JPEG optimization process!

The pot has been stirred, mixing in the ingredients.

And in the process, those pixels which *would* have had chromatic aberration have been *blended* with others from the safety paper background.

Might we have any hope, then, however small, of finding some "residue" of chromatic aberration? A chromatic aberration so small that we can't even see it with the naked eye?

Could it even be possible?

Maybe.

It's possible that even optimization might not erase *all* traces.

Using the computer to sample the digital color values from pixels could give us a much more accurate reading of the color than using our eyes alone.

What if we were to detect color values from the tops and bottoms of dark items in the color layer, and compare what we get? Might we find, on average, that the top pixels tend to shift color from the bottom pixels?

Using this theory, I sampled a bunch of pixels from the tops and bottoms of lines in the background image. I did this from half a dozen different locations in the image, to try and avoid the bias of sampling things from just one or a few areas.

The test I ran was a simple one: Check the color of a pixel on top of the line, then check one directly below it on the bottom of the line. Observe which direction the color shifted – towards red or towards blue – and keep track of the results.

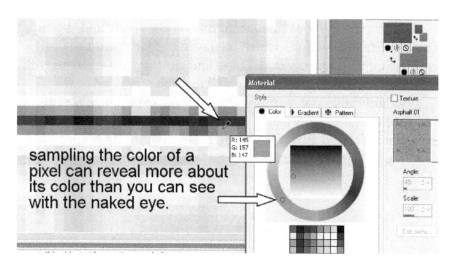

sampling the color of a pixel can reveal more about its color than you can see with the naked eye.

24 – Measuring Color Using the Computer

Most of the time, there was indeed some shift in color. However, it wasn't consistent as to whether it was up or down.

This was not at all unexpected. Any color variation at all in the safety paper would produce this. A bigger concern was that there were entire areas that seemed to go against the grain.

Nonetheless, a very slight pattern seemed to emerge – and it held in almost every single area from which I took samples.

The pixels on top of the lines tended to be slightly redder than the pixels on the bottom of the lines.

After sampling 255 pixel pairs in which I could detect a shift, 152 times, the pixels on top were redder, and 103 times, the pixels on the bottom were redder. At that point, I was reasonably confident in the result, and it seemed like a good stopping point.

The result does not constitute what I would call strong evidence. But it does, so far at least, indicate the likelihood of an apparent chromatic shift, and in the same direction as seen in the white-background AP scan – reddish on top, bluish on bottom.

Once again, what we find is completely consistent with our theory.

Our evidence could be strengthened, or weakened, by more comprehensive testing, which I haven't done because frankly, comparing these pixels is tedious, and 600 or 700 of them, with about 510 producing results, seemed enough.

So although not comprehensive, the experiment seems to indicate that, in accordance with all of our other evidence, the green-background PDF file did originate, before its optimization, from a photograph or a scan.

What's With the Mysterious White Halo?

"This particular type of white halo indicates, and how it appears in the layers indicate, again, that someone was attempting to enhance the clarity of the text in the document." [51]

– *Ivan Zatkovich, 16-page Report to WorldNetDaily*

In the last chapter, we began to get an idea of where at least *some* of our white halo might have come from: When solid-color items were "lifted off" into other layers, they were apparently replaced with plain white pixels. These then became blurred when the background JPEG was optimized.

However, since a small amount of white halo also appears around the grayscaled items that were "left behind," this alone does *not* seem to fully explain the entire phenomenon.

Before we investigate this mystery further, though, I'd like to make an observation about the white halo in general. Like so many of the other "odd" things we see in the PDF file, it has *no purpose* in a hand-created document.

What would it be good for? Like war (to recall the famous song from the 60s) – *absolutely nothing.*

The only "purpose" a white halo would serve in a forged document would be to create suspicion. Therefore, a forger would studiously avoid making such a halo.

And I say "making" such a halo because, once again, things like white halos don't just magically appear in computer graphics files put together by a human being.

They must be specifically and deliberately created by the person doing the graphics.

Was the Image Specifically Enhanced?

Ivan Zatkovich states that he believes the image may have been "enhanced." What he almost certainly means by this is *sharpened,* as a result of a human being giving a "sharpening" command to the computer, for the sake of clarity.

Computer graphics programs typically provide more than one way to "sharpen" an image. Here's an example in which a flat image with text in it has been "sharpened:"

25 – The Scanned Image May Also Have Been Sharpened

In the first line, the image has not been sharpened; in the second line, it has.

As Mr. Zatkovich seems to understand, sharpening an image can very well produce a white halo around it. And sharpening, as he's noted, can improve the clarity of an image.

How does this theory look in regard to the PDF? Frankly, it looks pretty good.

Working solely in Adobe Acrobat, I found I had better results in trying to duplicate the effects I saw if I first sharpened the image, and *then* optimized it.

So it appears to me that Ivan Zatkovich is correct in his statement that the image was most likely "enhanced" in this way.

This is, in fact, a far better explanation for the halo than human tampering. As we noted earlier, in order for a human being to introduce a white halo – apart from issuing a simple command like clarifying or optimizing the image – it would have to have been inserted quite deliberately.

Such an action (like so many of the things we see) would have been directly at cross purposes with the goal of a forger. It would have cost needless effort, and would only have increased scrutiny of the document, thus upping the chances that the forgery would be detected.

On the other hand, we have a very good explanation of how such a white halo arises through a human being telling the computer to run an automated process.

I Claim a $10,000 Prize

"These three u's, from three different places, are absolutely identical in their pixel mapping... I'm prepared to put out a challenge to anybody that can take a document, pre-1980, scan it and have any two letters be identical in their pixel mapping after blowing it up 1600%, like I've done here."

"So that's it. There's no question about it... the White House document of Barack Obama's long-form birth certificate is in fact a 100%, altered, fake, forged document. A pieced-together forgery." [52]

– "3TruthSeeker33," YouTube Video

In June, a YouTube user with the nickname of "3TruthSeeker33" posted a video entitled, *"Final Proof: Obama Birth Certificate a Fake, a Forgery, $10,000 Challenge!"*

3TruthSeeker33 clearly demonstrated in his video that three separate u's (the first "u" in the first "Honolulu," the "u" in "Oahu," and the second "u" in the second "Honolulu") were *identical* – right down to the pixel.

73

26 – The Three Identical u's Shown in the Video

He claimed that the duplicate letters were evidence of copying and pasting, and offered a $10,000 reward or prize to anybody who could otherwise duplicate the process and thereby prove him wrong:

"I am prepared to make an offer, a challenge, if you will, open to ANYONE who [will] take a typewritten document (i.e. a birth certificate printed on safety/security paper) from the 1960's, scan it at a high resolution, enlarge it 1600% in Adobe Photoshop, and find 3 of the same letters from various words within the document to turn out to be EXACT in their pixel mapping."

"I am talking about letter/number [sic] that appear originally in the document as is shown here in the Obama long-form birth certificate released by the White House April 27, 2011. If this can be duplicated through a verifiable process, I am prepared to personally pay $10,000 to the person who can do it."

3TruthSeeker33 concluded by writing, *"This is a serious challenge!"*

I happened across the video that afternoon, while doing a bit of research for this book. Since 3TruthSeeker33 specifically stated that his was a serious challenge, I did some further research, verified my ability to come up with such a document, and posted on his YouTube page that I was able to clearly demonstrate he was incorrect about the effect, adding:

"I can also conclusively show that this kind of pixel duplication can be and is routinely done without any kind of cut-and-paste forgery."

I ended my post with, "Therefore, with your kind permission and to the great benefit of my lovely family, I hereby claim the prize."

Beginning that evening, I exchanged a series of emails with 3TruthSeeker33.

Unfortunately, 3TruthSeeker33 never followed through on his promise to post the official rules. Apparently, he was not sincere in his offer. For our purposes, though, let's look at the proof I sent to 3TruthSeeker33, as to –

Why the Duplicated Letters Don't Mean Forgery

At first glance, the duplicated-letters phenomenon appears to be very suspicious. As in, really, *really* suspicious.

And it seems all the more so when you realize that two of the check boxes on the form are also identical, *right down to the pixel*.

These happen to be in a section where a box might be duplicated *if* the birth certificate were forged from a twin's birth certificate – and we *know of a set of twins who were born within days of Barack Obama*.

This was in fact the exact theory of one Internet blogger (the first to break the duplicate-letters story), who proclaimed positively that Barack Obama's birth certificate had been forged from that of one of the Nordyke twins – Susan or Gretchen, born on August 5, 1961, the day after Mr. Obama's reported date of birth.

In the summer of 2009, photos of the twins' long-form birth certificates were published in the *Honolulu Advertiser*. These images were later picked up by *WorldNetDaily*, and posted on their web site.[53]

When we begin to closely examine the Nordyke birth certificates, however, we run into problems.

If a forgery were done from one of their birth certificates, you would expect other things to line up – like the X's in the check boxes. And they simply don't.

Lots of Duplicate Letters

When our blogger who discovered the duplicate check boxes ("Miss Tickly") found that this phenomenon was not limited only to a few characters – but was present with *many* characters in the document – she was convinced that this meant the forgery was now proven beyond any doubt.[54]

How could all of these characters be duplicated, unless someone had made them that way? And in fact, it isn't terribly unusual for a graphic artist to copy one item to another.

My own initial reaction, on first hearing the news of the duplicate check boxes, was, "Holy cow!"

But as soon as it became apparent that the phenomenon was widespread, I knew that – far from being an indisputable confirmation – the duplication of so many characters was most likely going to prove fatal to the blogger's theory.

And the reason I knew this is that it would be extremely unlikely for a graphic artist to try to construct an entire document by scanning in individual characters and widely copying them.

Particularly, it would be even more unusual – and very difficult, in fact – for a graphic artist to try to reproduce an elaborate *form* by having *most* of the characters appear uniquely, but also to intersperse among these many more characters, that were hand-copied duplicates of others in the document.

And if the theory were true, then the *form itself* must have been constructed by this method – because that's where the vast majority of the character duplications are.

A Hand-Built Form?

Now there are only two ways that form construction like this could be done.

One way is that each letter could have been scanned individually, and then moved one by one to their appropriate places in the document.

Or, the entire form could have been scanned, with a graphic artist then deleting characters pretty much at random in order to replace them with hand copied characters.

But if someone is going to scan in a form, why go randomly deleting and replacing characters?

Either scenario would strongly risk detection of a forgery. And it would take an incredible amount of wasted time – especially when you consider that the end result had to be (and is) good enough to look like an authentic 1961 Hawaii birth certificate!

It would be far easier, and far safer, to simply scan in an authentic 1961 Hawaii birth certificate, and forge only the typewritten information regarding the specific child.

That would be the way that any *rational* forger would do it.

This theory, then, requires that our presumed graphic artist must pass up the opportunity to spend roughly 60 seconds scanning an actual form, in favor of spending literally days tediously constructing that same form by hand – and all at a hugely increased risk of having his forgery detected.

So once again, the *Graphic Artist* theory makes no sense.

A computer program, on the other hand, has a perfectly good reason for duplicating characters that appear to be alike.

In fact, there are several possible reasons for a computer program to behave this way. But let's focus on the single reason that I believe to be the correct one.

When a computer optimizes a file, it may be possible for it to save additional space by using a previously saved pattern of pixels.

If the program detects that a character is identical – or virtually identical – to one that it has already saved, then why use up extra space saving it again? Why not just make a note, "use this character?" And if, for example, one tenth of the characters in the scanned document can be handled this way, then the result is a pretty significant savings of space.

The Obama PDF file contains something more than 25 characters that are duplicated, including a great many of the "o"s. And this is perfectly consistent with the space-saving operation of a good optimization program.

In dealing with large graphic files over the web, saving space is the name of the game.

But Can We Find This Anywhere Else?

The skeptic will say, "Okay, nice theory. But can we find or create *other* documents that actually do this?"

Well, we previously discovered that many of the PDF documents in the Google Books library handled layers in the same way as the Obama birth certificate.

It turns out that they *also* show the exact same duplication of characters as that described by 3TruthSeeker33.

I will show you, in fact, a portion of the same page that I showed him. And I'll tell you where to find it, so that you may download the page and look for yourself.

Since 3TruthSeeker33 seemed to be interested in the truth, I began by searching Google Books for "truth."

You may have heard that truth is stranger than fiction. And it turns out that sometimes, it is.

If you would like to see the file I presented as evidence to 3TruthSeeker33, go to *books.google.com*, and search for "truth stranger than fiction." (You don't *have* to do this, however, as I'm including an image from the file here).

Your search should pull up an entire page of books with that title. Probably the first one in the list will be by a woman named Catharine Esther Beecher, published in the year 1850.

Once you've clicked on that, click the *Download* link to the right, and download the book in PDF format.

Open the downloaded file, and go to page 8 of the book. This shows a typewritten insert beginning with the words, "My dear Mr. James:"

Embedded in this one page, I found six identical "i"s, four identical "o"s, and three more "i"s that are also identical, but different from the first set.

You may be able to find other identical characters as well. I haven't made an exhaustive search, so I suspect I missed some.

Such characters are even more common in many of the Google Books files with normal (that is, not typewritten) print. This is because the printing-press letters tend to have less variation than typewritten ones.

Below is an image from this page. I have carefully copied the distinct letters marked, in the exact order marked.

Look closely. Notice anything similar?

27 – Duplicated Letters in "Truth Stranger Than Fiction"

Once again, our *Software Optimization* theory – the *only* theory that works – is completely consistent with *every* "oddity" in the PDF file that we observe.

What Do the "Different Sized Pixels" Mean?

"They've all been scaled 24% on the vertical and horizontally. But the last one is scaled 48%. Now if they had just imported one image and some software had run all this, they would have all been scaled an even amount. This one wouldn't have needed to be scaled double the size." [55]

– Albert Renshaw, YouTube Video

Albert Renshaw's "scaling" issue is directly related to the claim that the document contains different sized pixels.

As you can see in the illustration below, the pixels in the background layer do appear to be much larger than the pixels in the letters. Particularly note the little tiny blocks that stick out from the "p," the "r," and the "n," then look at the bigger squares that make up the background.

To be precise, each colored background square is twice as wide and twice as tall as any of the higher resolution pixels in the single color layers.

28 – The Background Is Scaled Differently

This is because the scaling for the background layer is twice as big as the scaling for any of the other layers. In Illustrator, as Albert Renshaw has noted, that shows up as "48%," versus "24%."

Because the background pixels are twice as big in both directions, the total area of a background pixel is four times the size of the other pixels (2 x 2 =4).

To Albert Renshaw, this seems to be proof of human intervention. He specifically says software wouldn't have done this.

But is he right?

I have worked with computer graphic editing software since at least the late 1990s. I cannot recall one single occasion on which I have ever deliberately scaled one layer to be a different pixel size from another layer.

In fact, if you want to simply present the most professional looking graphic, you would normally want to keep pixel sizes the same across all layers.

Once again, we have an effect that a forger would almost certainly take pains to avoid doing, because it would only work against his purpose of presenting a good forgery. He has nothing to gain by it.

And once again, we have an effect that a computer program *would* do, quite readily, for the sake of optimizing the PDF file.

Since the change in the scaling allows the program to cover the background with one *fourth* the number of pixels it would normally need, the program is able to save 75% of the space that would otherwise be required to store the background information.

If you've ever been to a 75% off sale, you can appreciate the savings involved.

Do We See This Elsewhere?

And guess what? We can also see the exact *same* effect in our optimized PDF files from Google Books! An example is below. (The illustration, by the way, is from the word "ears," in the *Tale of Little Red Riding Hood*, from *The Child's Wonder Book of Favourite Stories*.)

The area that Google Books keeps grayscaled has pixels that are four times the size – twice as wide and twice as tall – as the single color pixels of the black letters.

Again, this is because the optimizing program "knew" that the single color information would quite likely be text, and would therefore need smaller pixels in order to appear smooth.

29 – The Exact Same Scaling Scheme, in a Google Book

The goal with the smaller pixels is to keep the single-color layers high resolution. They're very "cheap" pixels, in terms of storage, since color information doesn't have to be stored for each pixel. We can use a *lot* of them and still keep the file size small.

Note here the single pixels sticking out at the bottom of the "r" and the top of the "s." Then compare these with the larger blocks from the right-hand portion of the image.

It's the exact same scaling as the Obama PDF: there are exactly 4 times as many solid-color pixels as there are of the much more expensive color ones.

Once again, everything fits.

WHY DO THE IMAGES SEEM ROTATED?

"The interesting thing about these links is they've all been... rotated negative 90 degrees... If you click on it, you can see the transformation they've applied after they imported it into Illustrator. This one was... rotated." [56]

— *Albert Renshaw, YouTube Video*

Albert Renshaw points out that, when you examine the single color images using Adobe Illustrator, they appear to have been rotated. He claims that this is evidence that a human being edited the document.

Now offhand, I can't think of a particular reason why a computer program would prefer to store the single color images in a rotated fashion. But then, there's no particular reason why a human being would, either.

As someone who works with computer graphics, I would normally rotate any extra scanned images that I wanted to incorporate *before* I imported them into my main graphic file.

I do this for the sake of comfort and convenience, and I think most other computer graphics people likely do the same.

While the human mind, under the right conditions, is easily capable of constructing the image a face from a pile of rocks on Mars (as we shall see later), it's much harder for humans to "see" what something is going to look like *after it is rotated*. It's a lot easier to just go ahead and rotate the item, and look at it that way.

But *these* images appear to have been rotated *after* being brought into the file. Rather odd behavior – for a human being.

Consistency Throughout All Elements

If we had a situation where some elements were rotated and others were not, that would definitely lend a bit of support to Albert's claim. We would not expect a computer program to be able to distinguish that some things should be rotated, and others should not be.

But that's *not* what we have. *All* of the elements, *including the background one*, appear to be equally rotated.

Perhaps this is an artifact of the document having been scanned on its side, and then "manually" rotated (by a human being issuing a "rotate" command to the computer program) just before it was optimized.

That sounds, in fact, much more likely than a human being deciding to manually rotate every single element in a file. And it's very common for people to scan documents, find they are sideways, and then rotate them.

In any event, however these elements became rotated, there doesn't seem to be any evidence here at all that would suggest element-by-element, manual human rotation over rotation by the action of a computer software program.

ODDITIES IN THE DATE STAMPS

"There are two different colors on both lines where there should be no color at all... the font size of the rubber stamp in box 22 is larger than the stamp used in box 20... this means these elements were taken from two separate forms that may have been years apart using different rubber stamps.[57]

— *Douglas Vogt, in His "Revised Affidavit"*

Douglas Vogt finds, in his words, "yet again another irrefutable proof this form is a forgery" in the color variations of the two registrar date stamps.

He also claims that the fonts are of two different sizes.

The Different Colored Date Stamps

There is indeed a variation in color within the registrar date stamps in the PDF file.

30 – The Two Date Stamps in the PDF Each Show Two Different Colors

Specifically, the "Date A," the "AUG – 8," and the "6" in "1961" are all green. All other letters and numbers are black.

However, no such variation in color appears in Savannah Guthrie's color photo.

This is a problem.

At least, it is for *Vogt's* theory. And it's one I can see no solution for – at all.

You Can't Get There From Here

The near-identical nature of the PDF and the Guthrie photos means that either one image was made from the other, or they were both made from the same source.

You can't get from the straight-gray stamps of Savannah Guthrie's photo to the mixed-color stamps of the PDF – at least, not without admitting that our theory, rather than Vogt's, is the correct one!

You also can't get from the mixed-color, low-resolution stamps of the PDF to Savannah Guthrie's calm, gray stamps on a higher-quality document. *At all.*

In that direction lies madness.

And you can't get from some third source to both – again, not without admitting that the PDF was processed by the computer, and that therefore, our *Software Optimization* theory is the right one.

Computers Don't Group Things Well

For *our* theory, there's no contradiction in the relationship between the documents, and no problem – since by now you will realize that the optimization software just wanted to pull all the text-type elements out into single-color layers, in order to keep things looking sharp while saving as much space as it could.

And it's just not as good at grouping the right things together as a human being would be.

In spite of the fact that IBM's *Watson* beat Ken Jennings at *Jeopardy!* earlier this year, we humans are still better at most things than our computers are.

For the time being, at least.

So how did our computer assistant go about this?

Well, not surprisingly, the main body of the form text (which was pretty much black) and the rubber date stamps (which are almost always a lighter color) were "pulled out" into *different* single-color layers.

Now it's important to realize here that documents (and particularly the marks left by rubber date stamps) are *not* uniformly the same color throughout. *We* hardly even notice the subtle variations of color. Our brains mostly ignore them.

But for a computer, they're a somewhat confusing problem.

All that's happened here is that the computer decided that it had some apparent text elements that looked like they were two different colors.

It then tried to gauge exactly what two colors it ought to use, and then forced all of the sharp-edged items it found into one of its two color categories.

In the date stamp in our illustration, the "19" and the "1" seemed particularly dark, so it said, "hey, these must be black." It took a guess; and on this particular occasion, it guessed wrong.

It found the "Date A" to be a problem, because computer programs still can't read terribly well, especially when the letters are all run together.

Well, actually, it didn't find the "Date A" at all.

What it *did* find was two *continuous blobs* of kinda mostly-dark pixels that sure looked like they needed to be made all one single color or the other. These blobs included the word "Date" run together with the letters "AU," and the letter "A" stuck to the letter "G."

And most of the pixels in these two blobs (or at least those that covered a bigger area) looked closer to the date-stamp color than the text color, so it made both of these blobs the green color instead of the almost-black one.

Which brings us to another problem for Vogt's theory.

Why exactly do we have three different shades of green and black on the date stamps, anyway? Even if they *did* come from different dates?

Do they just like using various colors of green ink at the Hawaii Department of Health? And is green the official color they use when stamping dates?

It certainly isn't the color on Savannah Guthrie's photograph.

Or... might it just possibly be that a *computer program* read the gray date stamps off of a green safety-paper background, then took some of what it saw of green, and some of what it saw of gray, and averaged it all to come up with a grayish green?

Vogt appears very much to be viewing the birth certificate through the eyes of someone who's already come to his conclusion, and is just looking for evidence to justify it.

In the process, he simply ignores all of the evidence against it.

Two Different Sized Fonts?

Douglas Vogt says,

"Finally the font size of the rubber stamp in box 22 is larger than the stamp used in box 20... Since we have two size letters and numbers, this means these elements were taken from two separate forms that may have been years apart using different rubber stamps."

Vogt makes this claim as an expert who expects to be taken seriously in a court of law – presumably, one that's going to charge the President of the United States with one or more felonies so that he may be impeached and removed from office.

Let's see how careful he has been to substantiate it.

Below is a graphic overlay that I made of the two stamps. The fact is, there is virtually no difference at all between the two!

31 – A Graphic Overlay of the Two Registrar Date Stamps

Not in the size of the characters. Not in the alignment of the characters, either – which there surely would be unless Vogt's forger were extremely, *extremely* careful... and if he were that careful, how could he possibly miss the fact that he was putting out a whole *kaleidoscope* of stamp colors?

In fact, looking at the illustration, it's probably not even immediately obvious that you're looking at two date stamps overlaid on top of each other. Even the gap between the "6" and the "1" matches with brutal precision.

The only possible conclusion, then, is that both date stamp marks came from either the *same* date stamp, or from two identical ones.

But since the less-than-perfect *vertical* alignment is identical in both cases – as well as the very slight slant to the rightmost "1" – I'd say the only *rational* conclusion is that the exact *same* date stamp was used in both places.

As for Vogt's claim that different font sizes are apparent – the claim is simply and obviously not true.

In fact, he must have recognized this himself, as it was mostly dropped from his *Final Affidavit*.

THE SCANNER WITH X-RAY VISION

"I have not seen anywhere... the simplest proof that it is a forgery: the overwhelming evidence provided by the presence of two 'white dot' groups in the image...

If the document were indeed scanned, there could not be varied green hues behind the white dots. No scanner has X-ray vision... No pixel can have two colors from a scanner." [58]

– Tom Harrison, WorldNetDaily Article

The idea here has to do with the two layers of white-colored "noise" that we mentioned very briefly back in our chapter on where the layers came from.

Since these were all white, and contained no significant content, we didn't illustrate them back in that chapter. But because they've been mentioned as another possible proof of fraud, we'll show them below. To make them easy to see, let's reverse their color and present them black-on-white.

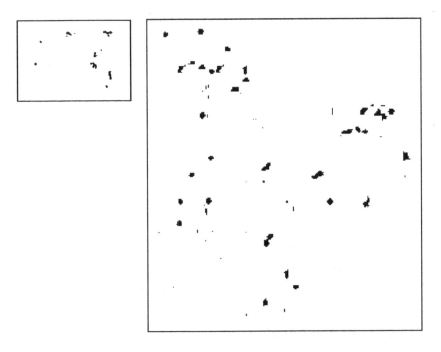

32 – The Two Groups of White "Noise" Pixels (Color Reversed)

Tom Harrison looked at the layer behind the white pixels – the multicolored background layer – and discovered there were varying shades of green behind these white pixels. His point is that "no scanner has X-ray vision." In other words, no scanner is capable of looking behind a white pixel and seeing whatever color of pixel might be behind it.

Therefore, he concludes, the document is a forgery.

Harrison's right that no scanner has X-ray vision. However, his idea that this is proof of fraud doesn't work – and for pretty much the same reasons as we've seen with other theories so far.

First, the *Graphic Artist* theory (which is what this is again) completely fails to tell us *why* the white "noise" pixels are there.

You will of course recall that if they were put there by a graphic artist or forger, then they had to have shown up for some reason. They don't just magically appear.

But why? As with similar theories, the person making the claim doesn't tell us this. He doesn't even attempt to.

The white pixels are another item that would represent completely wasted time and effort for a forger. Adding these two layers would only increase the risk of detection, operating directly against the forger's purposes.

Nor does there seem to be any reasonable scenario by which they might've appeared accidentally in the course of a forgery.

As before, each pixel has the exact same digital color value as every other pixel in its same layer. They have been pulled out by the optimizing software as items that the program thinks ought to be made all one color.

And while Harrison's theory comes up completely short on explanation, our theory has no difficulty in telling us why we see green pixels behind the white ones.

Optimizing a JPEG background layer – and this one clearly and indisputably was optimized as a JPEG – mixes up colors. This optimization has turned many of those pixels-behind-the-pixels varying shades of green.

Or, to be more precise:

First, the items that the program found suitable to pull out into high-resolution solid-color layers were "extracted."

Then, those pixels in the background layer – whatever their original color might have been – were replaced with safe white pixels.

Then, the background layer was optimized. This mixed the colors of that layer up a bit, exactly as we saw them mixed in the chapter on chromatic aberration. And when I tested the theory, the results were as predicted: varying shades of green pixels, that previously had been white.

Where Did The White Dots Come From?

Our explanation also reveals *why* we have the second set of pixels; and we can at least hazard a guess as to the reason for the first set.

The second (larger) group of white dots is located directly above the registrar date stamp.

It's located, in fact, *right on top of the seal.*

Now when you put a document with a raised seal into a scanner, the most-raised bits are going be pressed firmly against the glass. They're likely to be highly illuminated by the scanner's bright light, making them appear in the scan to be almost white in color.

It's pretty clear, then, why we have our second set of white pixels. They were separated out into their own layer because they were the brightest-reflected white bumps on the raised seal.

The other group of white dots is a bit more difficult to explain. There are only a few of them, and they're located along the top edge of the birth certificate, right in the middle.

Still, a reasonable explanation is not hard to imagine. Quite possibly there was a little bit of something white or reflective on the scanner glass – paper dust, a small amount of white correction fluid, smudges from a fingerprint, a bit of glue, or some debris from somebody's lunch.

Or perhaps there were little bits of dust on the *inside* of the scanner glass. Or maybe the safety paper pattern was simply brighter in that particular area for some reason.

Any of these is a plausible explanation for the small group of white dots at the top.

The idea that they provide clear evidence of a forgery, on the other hand, isn't.

No-One Has Duplicated
the PDF

"They'll put on an argument, like Kevin Davidson says this was the way the birth certificate was produced, and then he takes a piece of cardboard and he does some demonstration, and he says, 'Here, look at this.'

But he doesn't take the Obama birth certificate and produce a replication of the effects... by the computer techniques he's... describing as working.

And it has to be done not only so that Kevin Davidson can do that, but... so anybody can duplicate those techniques. When you really take a birth certificate and scan it, and run it through optimization, producing a PDF, it doesn't look anything like the Obama birth certificate...

Let's see the demonstration... And a replicable demonstration... He can't just boast, 'We gave an answer.'" [59]

– *Jerome Corsi, Interview with Ed Hale*

We've laid out an explanation that is in harmony with every known characteristic of the document. And in the testing of our explanation, we've actually duplicated – or at least shown where others have duplicated – most of the document's characteristics.

We've answered every single one of the many objections raised, while the *Graphic Artist* "proof-of-forgery" theory has repeatedly failed to do so.

However, we haven't identified all of the exact software used.

We do know, though – as Corsi acknowledges – that the PDF file was created on a Macintosh computer using Apple's Preview software.[60]

Although it's not particularly easy to tell, investigating further might give us a good idea of whether the person who saved the document used Preview alone to scan, rotate and optimize the birth certificate, or whether he or she just routed the image through Preview *after* scanning with some other program.

Since we haven't necessarily identified all of the exact software used, it should also be clear that we haven't pinpointed the exact settings.

But whatever the software and settings are, they appear to be very close – if not identical – to the software and settings that Google uses to optimize *Google Books.*

So why have I not precisely identified the exact software and settings? Well, it doesn't help that I don't actually own a Mac!

Still, we've been able to get pretty far without one.

I think it likely that someone (perhaps a reader of this book) will name the exact software and do the demonstration Corsi wants. In fact, the first person to solve that particular mystery – who clearly and convincingly demonstrates the solution via YouTube, that is then duplicated by others – will gain a mention on the *ObamaBirthBook* web site and, possibly, in a future edition of this book.

In the meantime, we still have enough evidence to understand the process that took place.

Does Not Duplicating the File Mean We're Wrong?

First of all, we've actually duplicated a surprising number of the effects shown in the PDF file; or clearly shown where someone else has duplicated them.

We haven't done this all in one demonstration, using an official Hawaii birth certificate, for the simple reason that we don't have access to the exact equipment and the original circumstances.

Dr. Corsi, and some others, would insist that we *must* give a live, replicable, exact-duplication demonstration in order to be able to determine that the effects observed aren't proofs of forgery.

But that's just not true, and here's why:

The Adobe PDF file format is and always has been, officially and in every other way, an *open* format. This means that Adobe *openly publishes* the recipe to tell people exactly how to create PDF files. And they've done so ever since PDF was first invented in 1993.

As a result, there are literally *dozens* of software programs that are capable of creating and/or manipulating PDF files.

So it isn't as simple as saying, "this would've been created using Adobe Acrobat." Acrobat is only *Adobe's* version of a program for working with PDF files.

And as we've seen, it's not even *their only* program! You can also open and work with PDF files in Adobe Illustrator as well.

But even if you're only using Acrobat, there are literally *billions* of different possible combinations just to optimize a PDF file.

And that, if anything, is an understatement.

So for anyone to claim that if we can't *exactly reproduce* absolutely *everything* we see, then it means that our theory must be wrong, is entirely without any basis in reality.

Or, to put it another way: there are *far more* possible combinations we might use to automatically modify this file than there are *people on the planet Earth.*

So if a failure to precisely duplicate everything in the document means a failure of our theory, then the police shouldn't be able to say that an unarmed man found in an alley shot six times was the victim of a murder... *unless* they can also pull in the *exact* person who shot him, in handcuffs.

And by the same token, those who push the *Graphic Artist* theory shouldn't be allowed to claim *that* belief, either, *even if they had the facts on their side* (which they don't) – until and unless they produce the exact forger, with a signed confession.

How About This?

To those who would claim that we must duplicate the document using the exact software and settings: Let's try this.

Why don't we take the same standard of proof that you want, and apply it to *your* theory?

Those who claim that the optimization and clarity-enhancing artifacts mentioned are proofs of forgery have never duplicated the file, either.

So... *you* produce a credible forgery, working by hand, showing *all* of the characteristics that we see in the Obama birth certificate PDF, *and that you claim are evidences of forgery.*

Every single one.

Go through this book, and make a complete list of all of the odd effects observed so far – from having bits and pieces of the form strewn across three layers, to the white halo around everything, to the "split" signature, to letters from the form itself (as well as its typed information) that are to-the-pixel duplicates.

I won't relist all of these characteristics here, as that would get a bit tedious.

But take the full list, and *manually produce* a document that meets *every one of these characteristics,* and to the degree and standards shown in the Obama certificate.

And once you've finished with that project – once you've successfully duplicated the document – *then you must clearly explain exactly why, as a forger, you chose to do all that you did in precisely this way.*

THE MYSTERIOUS SECOND FILE

"The White House has never acknowledged or explained why two different PDF versions of the Obama birth certificate were filed on the White House website." [61]

– Jerome Corsi, WorldNetDaily Article

This certainly seems disturbing, and suspicious.

Why on earth would the White House upload two different versions of the birth certificate file, if there wasn't something they wanted to "correct?"

Dr. Corsi produces as evidence an online post from someone with the nickname "weebles" – who points out that the PDF on the White House web site is different from the same file obtained indirectly via Douglas Vogt's web site, *www.archiveindex.com.* [62] Mr. Vogt's copy, which is 3K bigger, was reportedly downloaded by Vogt on April 28, the day after the original PDF was posted.

The very first question we ought to ask is, *"If the White House modified something in the file, what exactly was it – and why?"*

But a visual comparison of the two files shows no obvious difference at all. Hmm. So... *why the two different copies?*

Let's examine the differences we *can* compare, starting with the information provided by weebles.

Weebles reports – and I've confirmed – that the White House PDF shows only one date in it – "(D:20110427120924Z00'00)."

All of this is a computer abbreviation, and consulting Adobe's manual for PDF documents helps us fully decode it.[63] It says, "April 27, 2011, 12:09 and 24 seconds."

The "Z" and the zeroes that follow are a *time zone* marker. They indicate that the time shown is "Universal Time," or "UT."

This is what used to be called "Greenwich Mean Time." It's basically London time – *except* when the UK "leaps forward" for British Summer Time. And by April 27, 2011, they had.

What our time marker indicates, then, is that the file was created at 9 minutes past noon, Universal Time.

Now often, a date stamp like this reveals the time zone of the computer used. However, on April 27, 2011, nobody we know of was in Ireland, Iceland or West Africa – which were about the only places actually on "UT." We might therefore conclude that this particular file-creating software simply strips out the time zone info, adjusts the hour, and dates all files using Universal Time.

And in Washington, D.C., this was 8:09 a.m. on the morning of April 27th[64] – just over an hour and a half before the start of Mr. Obama's 9:45 a.m. press conference, in which he announced the release of the birth certificate.[65] So far, so good.

The second file lists this exact same date and time as the PDF's creation date. But it also has a *date and time that the file was modified.* And this reads: "2011-04-28T09:58:24-7:00."

Or, in plain English: "April 28, 9:58 a.m., and 24 seconds."

However... what's that "-7:00" on the end?

That's a time zone marker, too. It says "seven hours behind UT" – *and this one gives us the time zone of the computer that modified the file.* It thus reveals, roughly, the computer's *location.*

On the morning of April 28, 2011, Washington, D.C. is *not* seven hours behind Universal Time. But the United States West Coast – including Washington *State* – *is.*[66] And this reveals what happened: *It wasn't the White House* that modified the original PDF to produce our second version.

The file was modified – slightly and probably inadvertently – in Washington State... by Douglas B. Vogt.[67]

CONCLUSIONS REGARDING THE
WHITE HOUSE PDF

So far, we have observed the following things.

- We've seen that the size of the PDF file is 377 KB. This is about the same size as many *optimized* JPEG files that show similar sized images of decent quality. The fact that it is this small is an immediate and very clear indication that some kind of optimization has taken place.

- We've convincingly – if not conclusively – demonstrated that the official White House PDF, the AP white-background "photocopy" handout, and the photos posted by Savannah Guthrie are all images of the same original document.

We've confirmed that Guthrie's photos are of an actual, physical, paper document with a raised seal. And, we've noted that there is no difference whatsoever in any of the *information* printed on the three documents.

This alone is enough to tell us that the PDF file *cannot* have been altered in any meaningful way.

- We've shown that virtually none of the characteristics of the PDF file make any sense at all from the point of view of a human forger.

  Almost all of the oddities in the PDF file are things that a forger would actively *avoid* doing, because a) they serve no purpose, b) they cost time and effort, and c) they increase the risk of getting caught.

  In these oddities, we have found at least seven good reasons – entirely *aside* from the earlier evidence we gained from our two other documents – to reject the *Graphic Artist Theory*.[68]

- We've seen that, with the possible exception of the white halo and two small "neutral" oddities – the rotation of elements in the document and the slight shading/ blurring in the form area – *all* of the things we've observed make very *good* sense from the point of view of a computer software program optimizing the image. And the white halo makes very good sense from the point of view of enhancing image clarity.

- We've seen that even the two "neutral" oddities provide no evidence for a forgery. The rotation is consistent throughout *all* of the elements in the document, and can therefore be explained simply by someone having rotated the image. And the slight shading/ blurring of the PDF image (which is not well explained by any forgery theory), may well be an artifact from the scanner used.

- We've analyzed how and why the optimization was done, and we've seen exactly *how* it meets its goal – which is to make the file size smaller.

- We've seen that our evidence regarding chromatic aberration supports the idea that the document originated with a scan or a photo, and *not* as a hand-built graphic document.

- In summary, we should note that *every single oddity that we have any record of in the PDF file* can be fully accounted for by the simple theory that someone scanned an image, rotated and sharpened it, and optimized the PDF for the internet.

- And finally, we've even produced a large supply of *known* scanned and optimized documents from Google Books that show the exact same effects in terms of layers, combination of grayscaled and solid-color items, duplicated characters, and difference in scaling.

Having thoroughly investigated the matter in every respect that we could come up with, we've been able to find no good evidence at all – in regard to the characteristics of the PDF file itself – to support the idea that the file is a hand-built forgery.

Not one single point.

On the contrary, the evidence is pretty overwhelming that the PDF document – far from being hand-built by a human – *was simply optimized by the computer.*

CHARACTERISTICS OF THE DOCUMENT

Is "Kerning" Absolute Proof of a Fake?

"This intrusion into the space of this other letter... is called kerning. And this is what a printer or a computer does to make the appearance of letters more pleasing to the eye..."

*"A typewriter cannot do this because a typewriter is incapable of knowing what letter you're going to type next... To refute this point you must come up with a typewriter that contains a flux capacitor and thus is capable of accurately predicting the future... I think this case is closed." *[69]

– Karl Denninger, YouTube Video

Karl Denninger claims that the intrusion of two typewritten letters into each other's space on the Obama birth certificate is evidence of kerning. This, as Denninger notes, is a process of adjusting the spacing between characters to make things look better.

A good example is when a capital "V" and a capital "A" are moved closer together – because they fit better that way, and look better, too.

VAIL VAIL
unkerned   kerned

33 – Kerning Adjusts the Spacing of Letters to Make Them Look Better

Denninger rightly argues that a typewriter used in 1961 would not have had kerning capabilities, because it would not have been able to predict the next letter you were going to type. (Neither would it have been able to "hold" a letter until you struck the next key, allowing it to decide whether to kern a pair of letters.)

However, is the "intrusion" he refers to actually kerning, or is it simply the irregular spacing of an old typewriter?

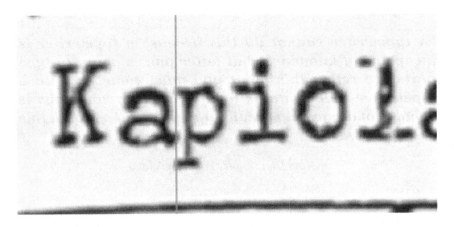

34 – Denninger Claims These Letters Intruding on Each Other Is "Kerning"

If this is kerning, it frankly seems to be a lousy job of it. The "a" and "p" are certainly close – but note the wide-looking spaces between the "o" and the two letters on either side of it.

There are plenty of other examples of uneven spacing in the document as well. Look at the spacing in the following word, "Honolulu:"

Honolulu₉

35 – The Word "Honolulu" Is Another Example of Uneven Spacing

Is Denninger seriously going to claim that the uneven spacing in this word is an example of sophisticated kerning designed to make the word look wonderful?

Look how close the "n" and the second "o" are to each other. Look how uneven this appears compared with the spacing between the first "o" and the "n."

Look how wide the gaps seem to be following both of the "l"s.

Clearly, this intrusion of one letter into the space of another (and note that it appears with that "n" and the second "o") is *not* kerning at all. *It is simply uneven spacing.* And far from being high technology, it isn't remotely sophisticated.

However, lest there remain the slightest bit of doubt, let's also consult the birth certificate of Edith Pauline Coats, born in Honolulu in June of 1962.[70]

Can we find anything similar on her birth certificate?

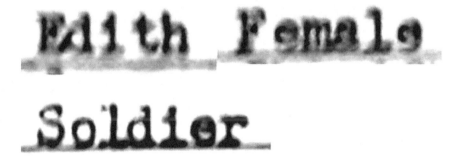

36 – Intrusion Of Letters in the 1962 Birth Certificate of Edith Coats

We don't have to look far: the very first two typed letters intrude on each other's space. These are the "E" and the "d" of "Edith." Note also the spacing in the last three letters of that word.

Then look at the irregular spacing, and the intrusion of letters, in the word "Female." We have a *huge* gap between the "F" and the "e," and then three letters so close that they look as if they're huddled together for warmth in a blizzard.

And look how the curve of the "d" on the second line, in the word "Soldier," intrudes into the space of the "l" before it.

This is the exact same effect that Denninger describes in Obama's birth certificate.

If he wants to continue making the claim, then, Mr. Denninger is not only going to first have to explain how the sometimes wildly uneven spacing supports his theory. Then, he's going to have to argue that Edith Pauline Coats' birth certificate must have been typed with a similar future-predicting typewriter – or that it must be a forgery, too.

Do Marks Align with "African Birth" Forgery?

> *"An analysis posted on Facebook by GoodTryBarry shows that markings on the Kenya document appear to be the same as markings on the White House release."* [71]
>
> – Dr. Jerome Corsi, WorldNetDaily Article

In the article quoted, Dr. Jerome Corsi asked,

"Could it be that the document released by the White House as President Obama's 'Certificate of Live Birth' from the state of Hawaii is linked with a well-known forgery that states Obama was born in Kenya and his Hawaiian birth was registered by his grandmother?"

Dr. Corsi then stated that the markings "appear to be the same" on both documents.

However, it is clear *even from the evidence presented in the article* that the markings – while similar – are *not* the same.

Dr. Corsi as much as acknowledged this in the article itself: *"The same marking appears in nearly the same location on the Kenya document on the right."*

"*Nearly* the same location" is not at all the same thing as "*in the same location.*"

In fact, all four items illustrated in the article were clearly different!

37 – The Marks Might Have Some Similarities, But They Are Clearly Different

These included:

- a hand written "2" which appeared in both documents (touching the line of the form in one document, but clearly *not* touching the line in the other, shown in our illustration)

- a claim that a scribble "covered up" double "X"s, when it quite clearly did not (on the right side of our illustration)

- markings that appeared to be two different characters, in roughly the same location on the two documents

- and the claim that the handwritten "X"s seen in the official Obama birth certificate also appeared on the forgery – when the visual evidence that was presented showed no such thing.

In fairness, the article also noted:

"A WND [WorldNetDaily] staff analysis concluded some of the markings also appear on the birth documents released earlier by the Nordyke twins, born at Kapiolani one day after Obama's reported birth at the same hospital."

"One suggestion is that when Hawaii moved to computerized records, a worker performing the data entry made similar markings on all original birth documents."

In fact, it's easy to see that similar handwritten notations appear both on the Nordyke twins' birth certificates, and on the 1963 birth certificate of a baby boy named "Alan." [72] Edith Coats' 1962 certificate also has what looks like a single similar marking.

I am not certain why Dr. Corsi published this article. One explanation might be that the article was the careless passing-along of completely invalid work by a semi-anonymous Facebook poster.

But do Dr. Corsi and *WorldNetDaily* not even check the information they pass along? It isn't even as if extensive checking was required.

You can tell just by *looking* that the points made by the original Facebook poster have little to no merit.

A Title with Innuendo

The title of the article is, *"Obama birth certificate linked to previous 'forgery'? Marks on White House image align with document claiming African birth."*

The quote marks around the word "forgery" appear to me to imply that the earlier document claiming Barack Obama was born in Africa just *might not* be a forgery after all.

However, the evidence in the article does not support that conclusion.

I have no problem with a journalist making an implication – *if* the evidence presented supports it.

But it doesn't.

At best, the claim presented in this article is misleading.

DOES A LACK OF TEXT CURVATURE MEAN FRAUD?

"The document appears to be... curved... Well, the print does not bend... So the print was superimposed on a template of a birth certificate..." [73]

> – Dr. Jerome Corsi, on the Tom Tancredo Show

"The conclusion you must come to is that the typed in form was superimposed over an existing original Certificate of Live Birth form." [74]

> – Douglas Vogt, "Final Affidavit"

"I've got a word that shows no evidence of actually having been on the page that was bent at the time that the paper was put onto the glass and copied. This was put on this document afterwards. There's absolutely no way you can possibly explain this happening, other than that." [75]

> – Karl Denninger, YouTube Video

The argument here is that the lines of the form curve, *but the lines of typed information regarding Barack Obama do not.*

Therefore, the Obama information was artificially added to the form, later, using a graphics program.

And Corsi, Vogt and Denninger are all in agreement on this point.

This particular allegation has the ring of one that might very well prove to be true – and that could signal the end of a Presidency.

In fact, Denninger calls it a "smoking gun that proves that this document is not authentic."

Let's test it and see whether it holds up under scrutiny.

Denninger's View

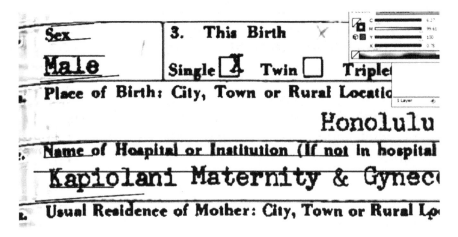

38 – Karl Denninger Argues that "Male" and "Kapiolani" Don't Curve

Denninger, Vogt, and Corsi make the claim that neither the word "Male" nor the word "Kapiolani" have any downward curve at the left, where they *should* curve downward *if they are part of the original document.*

The illustration above represents the situation according to Denninger. The only retouching I have done is to sharpen the contrast and redraw his lines in black, because I couldn't get his faint red lines to show up well enough to reproduce.

I have been extremely careful, however, to make the lines as nearly as possible *to-the-pixel* accurate to what Denninger shows in his video. Generally, his red lines were a bit wider. I have drawn my black ones straight down the middle of his, and with the exact same endpoints.

You can also see that the lines at top and bottom of "Male" and "Kapiolani" are level, just as they are in his video.

Upon looking closely at these words, we immediately begin to run into a bit of trouble. Look at the tops of the letters "a" and "e" in "Male." Compare the positions of the tops of these letters with the line above them.

If Denninger is correct, the top of the "a" should be at the same height as the top of the "e."

Or should it? Perhaps the "a" is naturally shorter.

Unfortunately, though, an examination of the "a" and the "e" in "Maternity" kills that theory. No, the tops of the "a" and the "e" *ought* to be level. And they aren't.

The "a" is lower.

The word "Maternity" *also* shows *another* troubling sign: The bottom of the "M" is slightly *higher* than the "a" next to it.

If that is how the "M" *normally* looks, then an "M" *on the same level* with the "a" would imply a drop to the left.

So comparing the "Male" with the "Mate" in "Maternity" leads us to believe that the "M" is, in fact, is positioned *lower* than the "a." And the "a" is positioned lower than the "e."

Which is exactly how they would be *if the curve that Denninger denies in fact exists.*

In fact, so far, every sign we've seen indicates that Denninger is likely wrong about the lack of a curve.

What about the positions of the *bottoms* of these letters?

Look at the bottom of the "a" and the "e." The "a" touches the line; the "e" is a pixel above it.

There seems to be no question here: on both the top and bottom of the letters, the "a" is *lower* than the "e."

Let's look at "Kapiolani."

Compare the tops of the "a," the "p", the "o" that follows, and finally, the "a" after that. Follow the line all the way out to the "e" and "c" in "Gynecological."

The line sits perfectly on the tops of the lower-case letters, from the "o" in "Kapiolani" all the way out.

But the "a" and the "p" are distinctly lower.

You can also see the slope in the top of the "K." And you can see it at the bottom of the letters "a," "p," and "i."

The "a" is firmly settled on the line. The "p" is slightly higher, barely touching. And the "i" is a pixel above.

In fact, it hardly seems necessary to draw our own image to demonstrate that Denninger is wrong. His own graphic is doing that for us, rather effectively.

Double-Checking, Using the AP Image

But perhaps the official PDF is a bit messed up. It's not the most detailed image we have. And we should double-check things, anyway. So let's see what happens if we draw some lines on the higher-quality AP image.

To get the best possible guides, I'm going to draw a first line on the straight part of the form, carefully, at the bottom of the typed line of characters, and as long and precise as possible. Then we will simply move and copy that line, making sure to keep things at the exact same original slope.

That will give us the best, most accurate lines we can get.

Male	Single	X Twin	Triplet	1st	2nd	3rd	Was Child Born Birth Date

Place of Birth: City, Town or Rural Location

Honolulu

Name of Hospital or Institution (If not in hospital or institution, give street add

Kapiolani Maternity & Gynecological Hospital

39 – Testing to See Whether the Curve Exists

Once again, we see the same things in the AP file as we saw in Denninger's image. The curve is slight, but it is *not* our imagination. It's there.

The top of the "M" is distinctly lower than the top of the "X."

The top of the "a" in "Male" is slightly lower than the top of the "e."

The bottom of the "M" is lower than the bottom of the "X."

In the "Kapiolani" line, the "M," the "G," and the "H" are all vertically aligned. The "K" is lower.

We still see the same drop of the "a" and the "p."

And just as the top of the "K" was lower than that of the other capitals, so it is with the bottom.

There are a couple of other tests we can run.

We can closely examine the "M" and the "K" to see whether it looks like the left side is lower than the right side.

While not 100% conclusive, it certainly appears that the left sides of these letters are lower than the right sides. We can see this in both documents.

We can also measure the distance from the "M" and the "K" to the line of the form, and compare that with the distance of other capitals from the line. This is not a definitive test, but we would suspect that if there's *no* curve, the "M" and "K" would be higher off of the line. They aren't.

Precisely measured, then, *all* of our tests – and I count 16 of them – agree:

There *is* a curve to the text, after all – and this slight curve seems to be in line with what we would expect if we were looking at an authentic document.

This proof of forgery fails, then – and we are going to have to keep looking for our one irrefutable evidence of fraud.

THE USE OF TAB STOPS

"1961 was the day of the typewriter, and nobody hand-centered things like that. Production typists used tab stops and if you look at other, known-authentic birth certificates from the time, you'll note that they're tab-aligned. Obama's is not..."

"Nobody <u>ever</u> manually centered or manually aligned production documents in a typewriter. Can that be explained? Maybe the janitor typed Obama's birth certificate." [76]

– Karl Denninger, Blog Post at Market-Ticker.org

Denninger claims that any typist in 1961 would have aligned the elements in the form by using tab stops. Yet Obama's isn't tab-stop-aligned. This would imply that the birth certificate was done much later... 2011, perhaps.

He has a point. Probably most typists in 1961 *would* have used tab stops, although I doubt we could say that they *all* would have.

A bit of research, however, reveals a very serious problem with Denninger's point.

Tab stops *were* used in the Hawaii birth certificates for Edith Pauline Coats (born June 1962), and "Alan" (last name unknown, born September 1963).[77]

However, they were *not* used for either Gretchen or Susan Nordyke, the twins born one day after Barack Obama's reported birth date, and reportedly, at the same hospital.

The alignment of elements in the two Nordyke certificates is a bit erratic. Most of the elements are centered; however, a few are roughly left-aligned or too far to the right.

The word "Caucasian" touches a line at left, similarly to the word "Kenya" in the Obama certificate.

Perhaps more tellingly, both the child's first name and the mother's street address seem to begin in a characteristic location – and the location is the same for all *three* certificates.

40 – Strong Similarities Suggest Same Typist for Nordyke Twins and Obama

This strongly suggests that the same typist who typed the Nordyke certificates – a somewhat unusual typist, at Kapiolani hospital, who preferred manually positioning things to using tab stops – also typed the Obama certificate.

And completely consistent with this theory is the fact that the date for the parent's signature on all three certificates appears to be in the exact same, distinctive handwriting, which is clearly different from the parent's handwriting on each certificate.

Is There an Official Seal?

"There's no seal. No seal." [78]

– Dr. Jerome Corsi, Interview with Alex Jones

A couple of weeks after making the above statement, Dr. Corsi was forced to backtrack, writing instead for *WorldNetDaily*:

"...the embossed seal on the Obama birth certificate released by the White House is visible only because a color filter was used to see it, otherwise it disappears in the design of the security paper." [79]

The accompanying image in that article is, I will admit, a better image than I had been able to extract with my own graphic enhancement. I'm not sure what color filter was used, but it did a good job.

Still, applying other enhancements had allowed me to independently pinpoint and circle the location of the seal. I then enhanced the same area from Savannah Guthrie's photo, and pasted that beside my "locator circle" in the PDF. Both images both show signs of a seal, and in the same location.

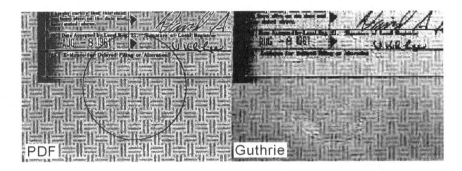

41 – A Faint Seal Appears on Both the PDF and Guthrie Images

Douglas Vogt makes a different claim in his *Final Affidavit:*

"The official seal on the Obama COLB is a second or even third generation image from another form. The seal embossing did not distort the lines or type on the form and it most likely was never part of his Certificate... Yet another indication this Certificate of Live Birth is an obvious forgery." [80]

Vogt claims to be able to tell, from a low-quality, optimized image, that the seal is completely flat. And oddly, he persists in making this claim even though he acknowledges Savannah Guthrie's personal statement that she saw the paper document and *felt* the raised seal!

Incidentally, Vogt also states that the seal is approximately 1-3/4 inches in size, and thus does not meet the legal standards in Hawaii for the size of seal to be used. In this, as far as I can tell, he appears to be correct. However, as Vogt himself admits, this does seem to be the size seal that the Department of Health is using.

Perhaps after the controversy, they will update their seal to conform more accurately to state law.

Vogt mentions having seen a seal on the birth certificate of Patricia Decosta that was the same size. [81] And further graphic comparison shows that the seal also appears to be the exact same size as the one on the birth certificate of Edith Pauline Coats.

Therefore, not only does the seal exist; its size is consistent with that which is visible on other known, valid Hawaii birth certificates.

DOES "HIDDEN TEXT" REVEAL A DIFFERENT NUMBER?

"Curiously, in a simple process run by Optical Character Recognition software that reveals hidden text, the registration number 10611 turns up, instead of 10641... The number 10611 would seem to be more plausible than 10641...

Is 10611 Obama's true birth registration number, the number on a document used by a forger or just a meaningless symbol beneath the text?" [82]

– Dr. Jerome Corsi, WorldNetDaily Article on "The Obama Code"

Dr. Corsi seems here to betray a lack of understanding of what Optical Character Recognition is.

He suggests that there may be hidden messages embedded in the birth certificate, that can then be revealed by OCR. In fact, the rather dramatic title of his article is: *"'The Obama Code': Hidden messages in birth document: Computer experts find anomalies embedded in White House release."*

But if you recall our earlier description of Optical Character Recognition, you may realize that there *is no* message "beneath the text."

All that Optical Character Recognition does is attempt to read the same image that you and I can see, and usually with much worse results.

The *exact process* that Corsi ran on the document – and I am drawing my information from the very graphic that Dr. Corsi himself features in his WorldNetDaily article – erroneously identifies "HEALTH" as "H1ALTH," "August" as "AUKUst," "Honolulu" as "11onolulu," and (I am not kidding here) "Kansas" as "anus."

There's no "Obama Code" here – only OCR misidentification.

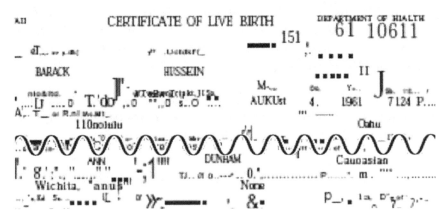

42 – Was the Certificate Really Issued by the Secretive "Department of H1alth?"

IS THIS THE CERTIFICATE
HAWAII SENT?

Some have questioned whether the certificate posted by the White House is the same document sent from the Department of Health in Hawaii.

We have a letter from Loretta J. Fuddy, Director of the Hawaii State Department of Health, attesting to the authenticity of the documents delivered to the White House.[83]

Of course, this doesn't necessarily mean that the document posted is the one that was sent.

However, in addition to a copy of a press release entitled, *"Hawaii Health Department Grants President Obama's Request for Certified Copies of 'Long Form' Birth Certificate,"* the Hawaii Department of Health web site also includes the following statement:

"On April 27, 2011 President Barack Obama posted a certified copy of his original Certificate of Live Birth. For information go to http://www.whitehouse.gov/blog/2011/04/27/president-obamas-long-form-birth-certificate." [84]

The link referenced is the official White House link announcing and presenting the release.

This pretty much amounts to an official confirmation from the State of Hawaii that the certificate posted by the White House is indeed what the Department of Health sent.

DID DR. FUKINO DESCRIBE
A DIFFERENT DOCUMENT?

"Fukino... wanted to inspect the files — and did so, taking with her the state official in charge of vital records. She found the original birth record, properly numbered, half typed and half hand-written, and signed by the doctor who delivered Obama, located in the files." [85]

– Michael Isikoff, NBC News

In an article touting "mounting evidence that president's document isn't genuine," *WorldNetDaily* noted,

"The document released by the White House was entirely typed. Only the signatures and two dates at the very bottom were 'handwritten.' What Fukino described is apparently a different document from what Obama released to the public." [86]

We should note a couple of things:

First, we have no direct quote at all from Dr. Fukino.

We simply have a description of what Michael Isikoff understood her to say – in Isikoff's choice of words. He does not directly quote her.

Secondly, the three signatures and the handwritten dates that accompany them do make up a significant portion of the content of the certificate.

I have seen copies of birth certificates from the era in which signature dates were typed, not handwritten. To say that the certificate is "half handwritten and half typed" is not an accurate statement, but it's not an extremely inaccurate one, either.

And anyone who has dealt even a small amount with reporters know that they do not always quote interviewees with 100% precision.

One can easily imagine a conversation along these lines:

Dr. Fukino: "Yes, it's a proper birth certificate, just like the others we have on file. They have a section at the top for the parents' information, and then down in the bottom half are all the signatures. That section has all the right signatures: the mother, the delivering doctor, and the registrar."

Isikoff: "Okay, let me get all this down." (Scribble, scribble.)

Without a direct quote from Dr. Fukino, Isikoff's description is weak evidence to suggest the possible existence of a different document – at best.

In addition – and probably even much more relevant – these certificates apparently contain an *additional section* at bottom, which is not available to the public. This is evident in the Nordyke certificates, where the bottom part has clearly been hidden with a piece of paper before copying to produce the certified copy.[87]

In fact, an article referenced elsewhere by Dr. Corsi states that *"the attending physician enters certain medical data [onto the certificate] and affixes his signature."* [88]

Since none of the certificate sections we can see contain any medical data at all – only the doctor's signature and date – we may safely assume that the bottom portion of the form that we can't see is where this data is recorded – *and it is most likely written in the handwriting of the physician.*

THE OUT-OF-SEQUENCE BIRTH CERTIFICATE NUMBER

"10641 is impossible to be Barack Obama's birth certificate number... When he was registered on August 8th, the number was stamped with an old one of the increment-by-number counters, '10641.' The Nordyke twins were born a day later in the hospital, August 5th. They were registered 3 days later, August 11th.

And they were given numbers 10637 and 10638. It's impossible, because that counter does not reverse. And 3-days-earlier registered Obama would've had to have a lower number, maybe by 20, from the Nordyke twins."[89]

– Jerome Corsi, Interview with Alex Jones

On a very ordinary work day back in the year 1961 – the same year that construction began on the Berlin Wall, John F. Kennedy was inaugurated as President, and the first disposable diapers in history landed on store shelves – an unknown file clerk in a very ordinary, obscure government office in the remote state of Hawaii stamped some very ordinary routine government paperwork, using a perfectly ordinary numbered stamp.

And there the matter was forgotten; not that it had ever been noted or regarded as important in the first place.

Not quite 50 years later, the stamping of those obscure and apparently unimportant documents would explode into a topic of national conversation.

Jerome Corsi and others have given detailed analysis as to why it is *"impossible"* for Barack Obama to have had the birth certificate number, "10641."

The key here is the birth certificate numbers of Gretchen and Susan Nordyke. The Nordyke twins were reportedly born one day after Barack Obama, and registered three days later than the registration date that appears on his certificate.

Let's clarify those reported dates:

- August 4, 1961: Barack Obama's date of birth

- August 5, 1961: the Nordykes twins' date of birth

- August 8, 1961: the Barack Obama certificate filing date

- August 11, 1961: the Nordyke twins certificate filing date

And yet Obama has the *higher* birth certificate number.

The Nordyke birth certificate numbers are 10637 (for Susan) and 10638 (for Gretchen). Obama's is 10641.

Jerome Corsi contends that it's "impossible" that someone simply stacked up a bunch of certificates, and stamped them in a rather random order, or that one batch was processed later than another batch – either of which would be a reasonable explanation for such a discrepancy in the order of the birth certificate numbers.

Specifically, Corsi claims (in a *WorldNetDaily* article dated May 16, 2011) that the certificate number would certainly have been assigned *on the day the certificate was accepted by the Registrar General.*[90]

The first thing we should note is that theories often fail in the light of what actually happens. Things get mislaid. Procedures aren't always followed to the letter. Or someone changes the procedure, with or without approval.

And we've actually seen a real-life example of this in the fact that the Hawaii Department of Health appears to be using a seal that's a slightly smaller size than that specified by State law.

But in this case, apparently, *none of the above needs to have happened at all.*

A False Claim Is Made to Support the Theory

In the above-referenced *WorldNetDaily* article, Corsi claims:

"... a 1955 article by Charles Bennett, Hawaii's registrar general in 1961, and George Tokuyama, chief of the registration and records section for the state's Department of Health, stated birth certificates were numbered immediately upon acceptance by the registrar-general..."

He then repeats the claim:

"Bennett's and Tokuyama's description of this procedure shows that birth certificates were numbered upon acceptance by the registrar-general, and there was no provision that would allow an accepted birth certificate to be put in a pile for three days before a number was stamped on it."

He then links to the original article ("Vital Records In Hawaii," *Hawaii Medical Journal,* Nov.–Dec. 1955).[91]

The major paragraphs describing the procedure of filing birth certificates are as follows:

"A nurse or clerk in the hospital fills in the certificate form and gets the mother to sign it. Then the attending physician enters certain medical data and affixes his signature. Finally, the hospital sends the completed certificate to the local registrar.

If any question arises relative to items in the certificate, the registrar usually asks the hospital about it rather than the attending physician. Nevertheless, the legal responsibility for reporting a birth remains with the physician."

And that's it.

In other words, there is not a single word in the article stating how birth certificates were numbered.

Based on the full article he himself has provided, Jerome Corsi's claim of what it says is simply untrue.

Enter Stig Waidelich

The same week that Barack Obama released his long-form birth certificate, CNN reporter Gary Tuchman went to the Hawaii Department of Health with a man named Stig Waidelich, who was born in Honolulu on August 5, 1961 – 13 hours after Barack Obama's reported date of birth.

The result of this visit was a short-form Certification of Live Birth for Mr. Waidelich, which showed his date of birth, and which revealed that his certificate was filed on August 8, 1961, the same day as the Barack Obama date.[92]

His certificate number, which was displayed on CNN, is 10920.

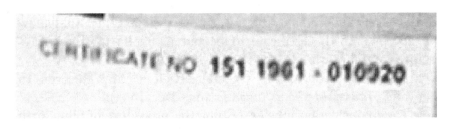

43 – Stig Waidelich's Birth Certificate Number Was Shown on CNN

Talk show host Teri O'Brien interviewed Dr. Jerome Corsi on June 5, 2011, inviting viewers beforehand to post questions for her guest. One of the questions, which included a link to a screenshot showing Waidelich's birth certificate number,[93] asked Dr. Corsi to respond to this issue. The issue, however, was not addressed.[94,95]

Waidelich's certificate number is roughly 280 numbers higher than the certificate numbers for both Obama and the Nordyke twins – and yet his certificate was filed the same day as Obama's, and three days before the Nordykes.

So what gives? Why the big discrepancy in certificate numbers?

Kevin Davidson, who runs *obamaconspiracy.org*, presents a theory that someone may have taken a batch of certificates representing roughly three weeks' work, alphabetized them, and stamped them that way. And he backs this theory up with some relevant calculations.[96]

I have independently run through the mathematics of this scenario. My numbers were very slightly different from Davidson's. But the end result was almost identical. And the mathematics of it turn out so uncannily accurate that the theory has to be taken seriously.

I would not be at all surprised to find that birth certificates were filed first by month, and then *alphabetically*.

If anyone makes a request for a birth certificate, how is the certificate going to be found? Not by certificate number, since the people making such requests almost always have no idea what the certificate number is.

Such a request is always along the lines of, "I'd like a copy of my birth certificate. My name at birth is Gretchen Nordyke, and I was born on August 5, 1961."

In any event, whether this is how it happened, or whether some of the certificates were simply shuffled around in a random order, there seems to be no escaping from the fact that Mr. Waidelich's birth certificate number is *far* more out of sequence than that of Mr. Obama.

And unless we somehow find convincing evidence to completely contradict this, the fact of this discrepancy – even if we had any evidence that Jerome Corsi was right about procedures, which we apparently don't – seems to totally invalidate the "out-of-sequence" fraud theory.

Was the Birth Certificate Number "Borrowed" from a Deceased Infant Born the Same Week?

There has also been speculation that Barack Obama's birth certificate number could have been "borrowed" from that of a deceased infant who was born the same week.[97]

An original Hawaii birth certificate (whether for this infant or any other person) bearing the exact same certificate number as that of Mr. Obama would obviously pose a major problem.

However, at this time, we have no hard evidence to substantiate this theory.

The suspicion in regard to a particular infant arose because of the out-of-sequence nature of the certificate numbers. The idea is that the particular little girl referred to, because of her birth date, *might* have had a birth certificate number of 10641.

But since Stig Waidelich's birth certificate number would seem to totally invalidate the "sequence fraud" theory (which was on shaky ground to start with due to no known evidence that certificates actually were stamped in order received) – and since we have no proof that Obama's certificate number was ever issued to any other person – this scenario is simply speculation.

"Certificate of Live Birth"

We have already dealt with this objection, briefly, at the beginning of the book. For the sake of completeness, though, I'll include it here with a bit more explanation.

It is important for the sake of vital records and public health statistics to distinguish between children who were born alive, and those who were stillborn. If the officials of a State know, for example, that they have an unusually high rate of stillbirths, then perhaps something can be done to improve the situation. And if they know that they have a very high survival rate for mothers and infants, then perhaps their practices can be shared with others.

In some States (although perhaps not in all), children who have been born alive are therefore issued a document called a "Certificate of Live Birth." And a different document is issued in regard to infants who are stillborn.

In fact, a US federal government panel on standard birth and death certificates, in April of 2000, referred to only two types of what we might call birth certificates: a "U.S. Standard Certificate of Live Birth," and a "U.S. Standard Report of Fetal Death." [98]

So, a Certificate of Live Birth *is* a birth certificate. That's the official name for it.

Hospitals may also issue a type of birth certificate, but the birth certificate needed for any and all official purposes is the one issued by the government.

DO DIFFERENT TYPEFACES
IRREFUTABLY PROVE FRAUD?

"My analysis proves beyond a doubt that it would be impossible for the different letters that appear in the Obama birth certificate to have been typed by one typewriter."

"Typewriters in 1961 could not change the size and shape of a letter on the fly like that. This document is definitely a forgery." [99]

– Paul Irey, WorldNetDaily Article

I begin the final chapter of this section not knowing for certain how it will end – because as I write this opening, I haven't done the analysis yet.

This chapter is going to be done completely on the fly.

Paul Irey's theory is independent of anything we have examined so far. *All of our other theories so far could fail, and this one could still provide us with quite convincing proof of a forgery.*

And it's a plausible theory.

Whether we can produce good evidence for it might turn out to be a different matter. But the theory itself is definitely worth investigating. And if the document were to be a forgery, this would be one of our very best possible avenues for detecting it.

So if we want to know the truth, as close as possible, this is an analysis that *has* to be done. Because this is where the rubber meets the road.

As we started out at the beginning of the book, so we are here: *We are not committed to a particular outcome.*

If we find that Irey's theory doesn't hold up, then we will report that.

On the other hand, if we find it does, we'll report that, too.

And if the theory *can* be substantiated, in a really convincing way, then *it could very well bring down the President of the United States.*

But *can* we find proof of fraud in the fonts?

Let's find out.

First, a Warning

I have to warn you that at this point the book is going to get pretty detailed for a little while.

I'd like to do this an easier way, but as far as I can tell, there's simply no way to get through the issue without getting down into the trenches and slugging it out.

A Couple of Possible Problems

From a first reading of the *WorldNetDaily* article, we can immediately spot two potential problems. However, these may not be fatal. We'll have to see.

The first problem is that Irey is attempting to do some sophisticated and delicate analysis of the fonts using a *fourth generation* copy.

The Associated Press document that he is using is:
    a photograph or a scan
        of a *photocopied* handout image
            of the certified paper copy
                of the original certificate in Hawaii.

Some of these steps are unavoidable, and some of them aren't that bad, in the sense that they shouldn't result in very much distortion. But the photocopy one might be a bit much.

Unfortunately, we don't at this time have access to better "original" images than the ones that we have.

But there *might* be a way to improve on these images a bit.

Our second problem is that the letters in Irey's chart show every sign of being distorted.

44 – Some of Irey's Letters Are Clearly Distorted

So Why the Distortion?

There are two major reasons for this: one that's largely unavoidable; and one that we most certainly *can* avoid.

The unavoidable reason is that photocopies often tend to have a bit of distortion. We'll have to work with, or around, that. Specifically, we have some other images we can consult: the PDF file and the two Guthrie photographs. And that may help.

The *avoidable* reason is that Irey (or someone) has "smoothed out" the images of the characters.

This kind of graphic "smoothing" is applied *as a normal measure* by most graphics programs whenever you enlarge an image. And it's done to make things nicer for us to look at. The smoothing makes the letters less jagged – but it also "hides" any distortion they came with in the first place.

Or to be more accurate, *it leaves the distortion there, but it disguises it from us – so that we might never realize that what we're looking at is distortion.*

It's not a good idea to try and reach *any* really important conclusions from distorted images – unless we're *crystal* clear as to exactly how much distortion we have.

We will therefore do our best to avoid smoothing these images out. This will require deliberately overriding the smoothing in any images that we enlarge.

Our Building Blocks Are Too Big

Let's look at an example, so that you further can see what I'm talking about. Believe it or not, the images below are all of the *exact same character* from the *exact same paper document* – the first "c" in "Gynecological."

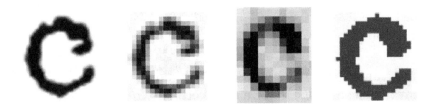

45 – Smoothing The Graphic Adds Detail That Isn't There

The first image is Paul Irey's. The second is how it appears on the original AP image he took it from. (See how much false "detail" the smoothing adds?)

The third image is how the exact same character appears – after contrast adjustments – in Savannah Guthrie's photograph. And the fourth is how it appears in the White House PDF.

Irey's image makes the flaws, distortions and pixelation of the photocopy look like characteristics of the font. But we can't just take a rough image, apply graphic smoothing, and then claim that what we have is an accurate representation of the underlying character.

On the other hand, the Guthrie photograph is low resolution, and the White House PDF eliminates all gray shades. So what are we to do?

Putting Our Information to Use

We have grayscaled information in two separate files: the AP document and the Guthrie photograph. But the blocks are too big.

But what if we were able to somehow combine the two files? Might the two files "averaged together," without smoothing, help correct some of each other's flaws?

I use the word "some" because certainly not all distortions would be overridden. But at least it might help us see where the differences lie, and we would probably come closer to the truth by choosing the middle path between the two than by simply using either file by itself.

The darker pixels from one image *should* combine with the differently-scaled darker pixels in the other image to produce a somewhat more accurate composite. The different bits of information ought to reinforce each other.

For all of these reasons, I decided to overlay the characters that appear in the two different documents. Hours of delicate graphics work produced five pages of images. The first page is shown below.

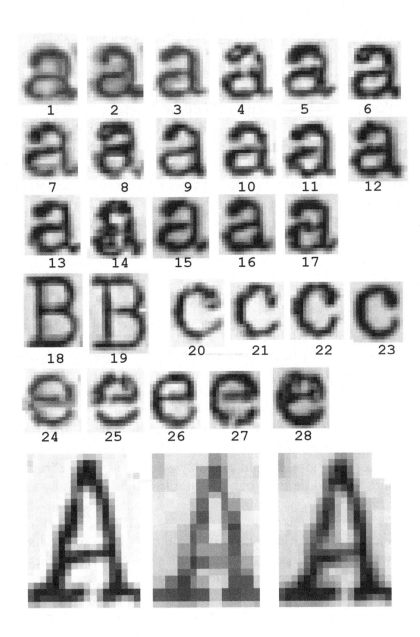

46 – Some Distortions Can Be Seen Even in Combined Images

Because our higher-resolution photo from Savannah Guthrie only shows part of the document, and because 13 letters only occur one time each – so there's nothing to compare them to – we have a total of 145 characters.[100] That's almost 100 fewer than Irey's set, but it will probably be enough – especially when we go back and reevaluate *his* work as well.

A Plan of Action

Now it should be clear that even our merged images still contain distortions. You can't begin with distorted characters, and end up distortion-free.

Look, for example, at the enlarged capital "A" at the bottom of the first set of images. The three figures are, from left to right:

- the letter as it appears in the AP photocopy image
- the letter as it appears in the Guthrie photograph
- and our merged version containing the information from *both* sources

There's no font on the market (there might possibly be now as a novelty, but certainly not for office use in 1961) with capital "A"s that sag in at the left, bulge outward at the right, and slant the bar up from left to right.

So we will need to be careful in evaluating even our combined images.

By the way, this letter is the final capital "A" in the Guthrie photo – the "A" in "DUNHAM."

The "c" that we just looked at in a distorted form in Irey's image is the first of four c's in our set of images (item 20). While we can still see the white gap at the top that came from a flaw in the photocopy, it now seems reasonably clear that this part *ought* to look like the third and fourth c's. However, the bottom part still looks as if it might possibly be curved a bit differently.

A bit of thought gives us a method by which we can proceed.

First, we'll investigate any suspicious characters on our own list. Then, we'll go back and check Paul Irey's work, referring to our combined images as well as to the three original sources.

Where Inconsistencies and Distortions Come From

In order to understand what our characters mean, it may help to list where inconsistencies and distortions are likely to come from. These might be the result of:

- variations in keystroke pressure and speed by the typist

- inconsistencies in the typewriter ribbon and ink

- inconsistencies in the paper texture and ink absorbency

- being two to three generations of duplication away from the original (including any issues with photocopy quality)

- and drawing characters using a limited number of pixels.

That's quite a bit of room for error. But fortunately, we have multiple sources of information. That's going to help.

A look through our five pages of images will give us a list of suspicious characters. On our first page, these are the ones numbered 1, 16, 17, 21, and 26.

Straight into a Problem

The very first "a" (our item number 1) presents a problem – again, not for us, but for the theory we're investigating.

The AP and Guthrie images of this letter are so different that they can't really even be merged to make one cohesive image. The AP image (which is the one Irey's using) is a *lot* wider.

What on earth happened here?

A close examination of the AP document reveals that Paul Irey has missed something extraordinarily important to his analysis. And it's going to hurt his theory badly.

There are two lines of photocopier-caused distortion running vertically for most of the length of the page.

The distortion causes a straight, horizontal "gash" between the letters "a" and "l" of "Male," at the bottom of the letters.

A second ripple of distortion affects the letter "e" as well.

Male

47 – A Horizontal Gash is Visible Between the "a" and the "l"

The two vertical ripples continue down the page, warping many of the typewritten and form letters along the left side of the page. And *between* the two "stretch zones," it *compresses* the letters slightly, as seen in the e's of "Place," "Name" and "stated," and the "s" in "best." Below, dashes show where the vertical stretch zones are, and the compression zone is between the two vertical ripples.

This also affects the date stamp a bit. We didn't notice this earlier when working with the date stamps, because we were using the PDF image, not the photocopy one.

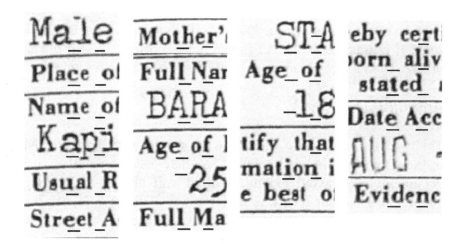

48 – Characters (Including Form Letters) Affected by Ripples of Distortion

Below is an illustration showing the approximate location of the entire "ripple zone" (stretch-compress-stretch).[101]

Sex		3. This Birth			4. If Twin or Triplet, Was Child Born			5a. Birth Date
Ma		Single ☒ Twin ☐	Triplet ☐		1st ☐ 2nd ☐	3rd ☐		

Place of Birth: City, Town or Rural Location

Honolulu

Name of Hospital or Institution (If not in hospital or institution, give street addre

Ka iolani Maternity & Gynecological Hospital

Full name of Father

BARACK   HUSSEIN   OE

Age Father	11. Birthplace (Island, State or Foreign Country)	12a. Usual Occupatic
5	Kenya, East Africa	Studer

Full Maiden Name of Mother

STANLEY   ANN   DUNE

49 – The Location of Our "Ripple Zone" of Distortion

Our first "a," the one from "Kapiolani," comes from this ripple zone. It is warped in the AP image but is normal in both of the others. Therefore, we can cross it off of our list of suspect letters.

Anything Definite?

The two "a"s in "Kansas" (items 16 and 17) appear a bit distorted in the photocopy, but reasonably like other "a"s in our other two documents. (To avoid extending what will already be a long chapter, I leave out illustrations for a few of these comparisons and refer interested readers to the original PDF and AP images.)[102]

The first "c" in "Gynecological" (item 20, mentioned earlier) seems to have a bit of its curved edge missing from the lower right. This can easily be attributed to an ink or ribbon issue or a paper irregularity. The second "c" (item 21) looks a bit different in the photocopy version. However, the difference isn't nearly as clear in the Guthrie or PDF documents.

Not in the C's

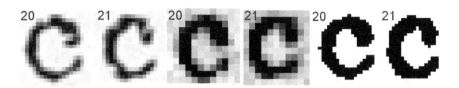

50 – AP, Guthrie, and PDF Views of the Two "C"s in "Gynecological"

We're actually comparing the second "c" here with the first one. This is the one that Irey presents in its distorted form, and the one we've just ruled out.

There seems to be something else going on in the photocopy that isn't going on in the other two – something with this second "c" – so we really have to rely mostly on the Guthrie and PDF views. And these don't make plain any theory that the "c"s are from different fonts. In the highly-pixellated Guthrie view, the first "c" seems a bit thinner. In the PDF, they seem about the same.

When we consult all four "c"s in a row (items 20-23), it's still not entirely clear whether they have the same shape or not. There's just too much distortion to really be able to tell with certainty.

The "Scrunched" "e"

The "e" in "Kalanianaole" (item number 26 on our combined-character list) also seems a bit scrunched at the right. And while the effect might possibly be exaggerated in the photocopy, it doesn't seem to be entirely isolated there.

Whatever has caused this scrunched look – distortions in the original document, ink irregularities, or a different typeface – it looks as if it might be at least slightly visible in Guthrie's photo and the PDF as well.

Hmm.

At this point, then, we are going to leave our ivory tower of dealing with the images alone, and go do some typeface research –

in order to see if we can discover *any* 1960-era type style that has a right-flattened "e."

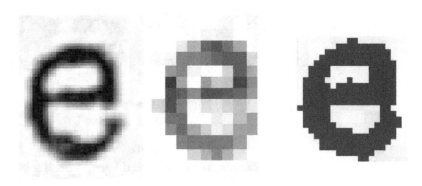

51 – A Slightly "Scrunched" e? Views From AP, Guthrie and the PDF

Into the Jungle of Mid-20th-Century Typography

Many hours and 332 type styles later – the major typewriter manufacturers had a surprisingly large inventory – we know a bit more.[103]

We know from a careful visual comparison that the typefaces on the Obama, Nordyke, Coats, and "Alan" [104] birth certificates (1961-1963), even though they list three different hospitals, are extraordinarily similar if not identical.

It may well be that there was one major provider of typewriters for hospitals in Honolulu in the late 1950s and early 1960s, and that provider usually sold a particular line of typewriters with a specific standard font.

We know that the font looks a lot like some of the variations of Pica or Elite, and that it is very similar to some of the Elite styles from Remington, Olivetti, Smith Corona, and IBM.

Pica and Elite were huge in those days.

REMINGTON ELITE, 504-12 pitch is app:
for business and personal correspon¢
for duplicating work, labeling, med:
prescriptions. 1234567890

OLIVETTI DISTINCTIVE ELITE 12 Pitch 6 lines to an inch

This is a sample of Distinctive
Your particular typing applicatic
requirements. May we assist you
most suitable type style for you:
ABCDEFGHIJKLMNOPQRSTUVWXYZ !@#
abcdefghijklmnopqrstuvwxyz 123,

Smith-Corona

Elite No. 66
12 Characters
per inch
6 lines to
a vertical inch
Deluxe Electric
Standard, Electric
Deluxe Manual

Code 023
12 Pitch

Type

Widely used for general
one of the most popular
much typewritten materia
giving a crowded appeara
for forms, reports, and
with clarity and sharpne
ABCDEFGHIJKLMNOPQRSTUVWX
abcdefghijklmnopqrstuvwx

IBM Cloister Elite
good carbon copies
asdfghjkl;'zxcvbnn

52 – The Font Is Similar to Elite Type Styles From Major Manufacturers

And we also know that we don't have any *good* evidence that this "e" is from a different font. Is it possible that it *could* be? Yes. But it could equally well come simply from a small distortion in either the original birth certificate or its certified copy. This might be caused by unevenness in the paper, a speck of grime, sawdust or fluff between the paper and the roll, an odd movement of the carriage, an optical glitch in scanning the original... there are many possibilities.

Addressing Our Other Suspects, One by One

The "A" in "DUNHAM," along with its other distortions in our merged image, has a bar that seems to slant upward (see item number 37 below).

But it doesn't look that way in either the Guthrie or PDF images. That, then, is a slight optical distortion in the photocopy.

The capital "E"s, when compared across all documents, don't look quite identical. However, this can easily be simply because the "E" in "East" (item number 40) was struck a bit harder than the other two.

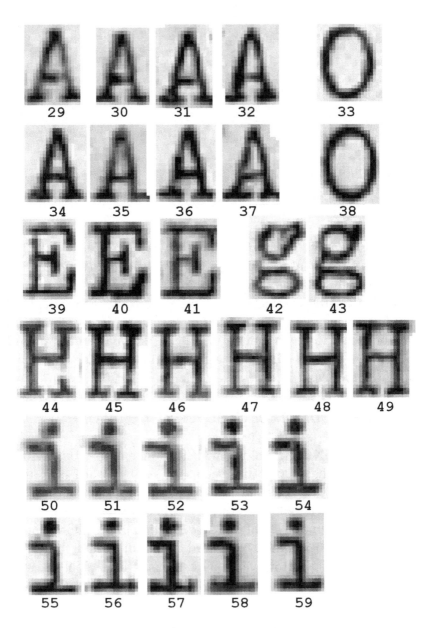

53 – Second Set of Combined Images

There's no "g," in *any* font, that looks like our item number 42. Period. It's a obviously a poster child for distortion. And when viewed in the PDF, the two different "g"s, aside from a blob of ink in the top of the first, look very similar.

There's no compelling proof in the "i"s (50 through 59). A possible difference, but no proof of it.

The "K" in "Kapiolani" (item 60 below) is on the curve, and slanted down to the left. This explains why it looks a bit different.

The l's of items 71 and 74 look like they didn't strike the page well at the top. Item number 75, (which represents the "1" in "18") seems to be shorter at the top and bottom left.

But then, it *should* be. It's in the ripple distortion zone, as clearly seen by the left-shortened "T" of "STANLEY" directly above it (a view of this character is in Illustration 48).

Incidentally, there's *no* non-italic, non-cursive office business font, particularly in 1961, that has a non-symmetrical capital "T," like the one shown there.

The "l" and the "T" both look normal in the other images.

The "p" of item 95 is in the "compression area" in the middle of the ripple zone. The two p's (95 and 96) still look slightly different in the Guthrie and PDF images (with the second one looking slightly larger), but there's no apparent style difference. And the differences we do see aren't anything we couldn't put down to our causes of variation, plus the fact that the first "p" is on the book curve we detected earlier.

And because of this, it is probably slightly farther away from the camera.

The "N" in "STANLEY"

This brings us to the "N" in "STANLEY" (item 98).

For whatever reason, it seems to be missing part of its "platform" at the upper left.

However, an examination of all three of our source images shows that the "N" is spotty and a bit faint. This could be the reason.

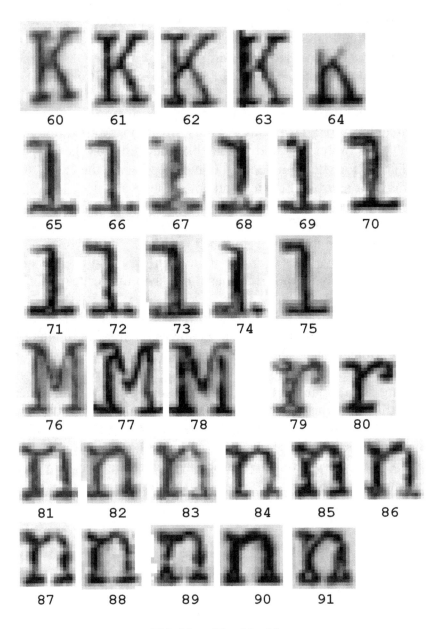

54 – Third Set of Combined Images

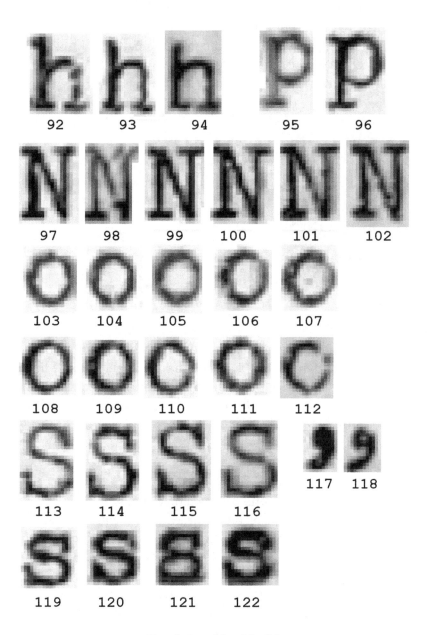

92   93   94   95   96

97   98   99   100   101   102

103   104   105   106   107

108   109   110   111   112

113   114   115   116   117   118

119   120   121   122

55 – Fourth Set of Combined Images

In fact, our "N"s numbered 97 and 102 look well-struck; number 99 through 101 look not quite as well-struck, and number 98 (the one we're looking at) seems as if it could be a better example of the fading effect we can see in 99 through 101.

A bit of extra graphics work may help us out here.

Drawing the slope of the lines allows us to project where the top of the "N" should be.

56 – Solving the "N"

It's obvious from our lines that in order for the problem at the top to be due to a different font, we *must* have a "bend" in the line of the "N." Since we won't find that in any mid-20th-century office font, we may safely conclude that the anomaly at the top of our "N" is due simply to a light strike.

The Last Item

This brings us to our "t"s, the last item on our list.

Having looked at all of our sources of information on these characters, it seems impossible to state with certainty whether some might come from slightly different fonts, or whether they are all the same typeface varied only by the factors listed earlier.

Out of our 145 characters, then, we have several – an "e" (26), a couple of "i"s (maybe 51 and 56) and a few "t"s (possibly 123, 124, and 126) that *might* come from different fonts – but just as well might not. Given our list of possible causes of variation, I find this well within the range of what we might expect to see.

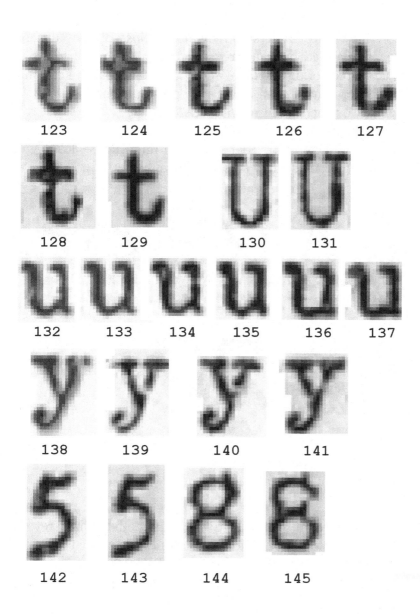

57 – Final Set of Combined Images

Double-Checking Paul Irey

As you may have understood by now, *most* of the "different typefaces" claimed by Paul Irey can easily be explained by our various sources of distortion – and by the fact that in smoothing the characters rather than leaving the pixel information in, he has (knowingly or not) *disguised those distortions.*

Let's double-check his list.[105]

Irey's character pairs that still seem important – leaving out those we've already dealt with – are shown below.

(Numbers are from Paul Irey's system, not ours.)

58 – These Seem to Be Irey's Most Important Remaining Character Pairs

We have already addressed the two "t"s in "student" that Irey uses as prime examples; but it's worth mentioning again that these look less convincing in both the Guthrie and PDF images.

So we are left with a total of five character pairs. Let's look at these in order.

A Pattern Begins to Emerge

We begin with the two "A"s in the second "BARACK." The first of these looks wider, the second more narrow.

And yet when we look at the Guthrie image, we find that the *opposite*, very slightly, is true. Here, it's the *second* "A" that looks as if it might be just a hair fatter! What gives?

"What gives" is two things: first, the slanted sides of the "A"s are very difficult for vertically-oriented square pixels to deal with accurately – particularly if the pixels are limited. That explains the slight difference in the Guthrie photo.

But why the *opposite* difference in the photocopy? Very simple. *The first of these characters is right on the ripple zone, and is therefore warped.*

Okay, first set of characters down.

Incidentally, there's an "R" between these two that is clearly affected as well.

Not surprisingly, we find that exact "R" as one of the next two characters on our list! And a comparison of the two "R"s using the PDF finds no real difference in their shape.

A Slanted-Bar "e"?

Our next odd character is the "e" in "Male."

Like the "K" in "Kapiolani," it's on the slope of the curve, which is probably enough to explain the strange-looking slanted bar. And it's in the second wave of the ripple zone as well, which appears to have made it roughly a pixel wider than it otherwise would've been.

In addition, reviewing more than a *hundred* fairly similar typewriter fonts from all the major manufacturers of the era, I was able to find only *one* font with a slanted-bar "e" that looked somewhat similar – and its curve was different.

Is it *possible* this character could be from a different font? Yes, but it seems very unlikely. Its position both on the curve and in the ripple zone, and the apparent lack of any major matching font from the era, are quite telling.

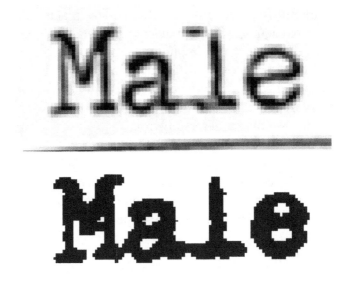

59 – The "e" in "Male" Is Both on the Curve and at the Ripple Zone

The Final Items

Next (and almost last) are the two "n"s from "Kapiolani" and "University." Irey maintains that these are clearly different sizes.
Here's what they look like in the PDF:

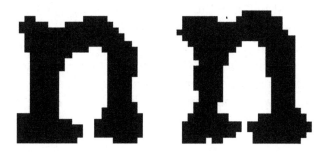

60 – The Heights of Our Most Different "n"s Are Only 1 Pixel Different

The height of these two letters is only a single pixel "different" – and this is probably because of variances in the typist's strike and the dynamics of the inked ribbon against the paper.

The final item on our list is the pair of "2"s. Just looking at them on Irey's chart, the second one looks distorted, but still I felt this was one of his best examples. They look like this in the PDF:

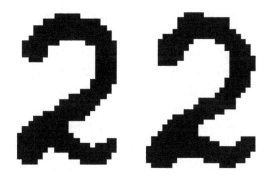

61 – The "2"s that Irey Gives as Evidence, From the PDF

So why do they look so different as presented by Paul Irey?

The second one is the "2" in "25." Like so many of these characters, it comes from the exact same infamous area in the AP photocopy. And just like the "o" in the word "of" just above it, it's warped and possibly a bit compressed.

So once again – for the fourth time in five character pairs – Paul Irey has fallen victim to the ripple zone – *and to a lack of cross-checking with our other two documents.*

And these were the items I picked out as being Irey's best examples.

Conclusion

It has taken more than two days' work, and some 24 pages, to do a detailed examination of the typewritten characters in Obama's birth certificate, to see whether any might come from different fonts. *But we've done it.* And we have learned a *lot* in the process.

I respect Paul Irey's typography experience, and I definitely respect his having started a company and built it to 60 employees.

However, typography by itself won't bring us to an accurate conclusion here. We have to look carefully at *all* of the best information we have, in the context that we have it – including a careful assessment of how far we can actually go on the information available.

And after a careful examination, Irey's analysis hangs in tatters. It has been pulled down by the weight of the photocopying and pixel-related distortions.

In the end, we are left with just a scant handful out of 244 characters – the half dozen we counted earlier and *maybe* a couple of the "c"s – that now seem as if they *might* – or, on the other hand, just as well *might not* – come from different fonts.[106]

The fonts, however, will prove meaningless if we can find a significant problem in the document's actual information. Some of the claims in this area are likely to be weak, but we might be able to come up with a "smoking gun."

So, let us see what we can discover there.

THE DOCUMENT'S INFORMATION

"TXE" SMOKING GUN

"I want just a quick simple way to show people how comical this fraud is. You know, I've shown that the state registrar's stamp has a misspelling in it. Instead of 'THE RECORD,' it's 'T-X-E RECORD.' Now nobody uses a stamp with a misspelling in it." [107]

– Dr. Jerome Corsi, Interview with Alex Jones

Jerome Corsi (and many others) have claimed that the certifying registrar's stamp states, "I CERTIFY THIS IS A TRUE COPY OR ABSTRACT OF TXE RECORD ON FILE..."

The Guthrie photo is too low-resolution to tell us much, but a close examination of the PDF and AP documents will help us get to the bottom of the "TXE" issue.

In both of these, we see a clear thickening of a whole string of letters in the second line of the stamp.

This starts with the "C" in "ABSTRACT" (and possibly with the "A" before it), and goes through the "E" in "THE."

TIFY THIS IS A TI

RACT OF THE RI

HAWAII STATE D

TIFY THIS IS A TI

RACT OF THE RI

HAWAII STATE D

62 – The Entire Area of the Claimed "TXE," in the AP and PDF Documents

The most likely cause of this thickening of letters is a partial deterioration of the rubber in the stamp.

A couple of other factors might also come into play, including the amount of ink at that part of the stamp, the amount of pressure there, and so forth. But the obvious explanation is simply that the stamp is not in the best condition.

This idea is further supported by the fact that *all five* of the letters in the words "OF THE" have sketchiness and gaps in them (see the top image in the illustration).

It seems particularly evident when you look at the blown up image of the AP document that what we see here is not a misspelling at all, but simply problems with gaps in the letter "H."

63 – The "X" Has Apparent Signs of Straight Shading on the Right Side

Aside from showing gaps in the "T" and the "E," the image has a faint straight line down the right side of the letter. This is completely consistent with its being an "H," and *should not* be there if the letter is an "X."

Further evidence that the stamp is not in particularly good shape can be seen in the final "H" in "HEALTH," the "A" in "Alvin," the second "a" in "Onaka," the "P" in "Ph.D.," and the "A" in "REGISTRAR."

I CERTIFY THIS IS A TRUE COPY OR
ABSTRACT OF THE RECORD ON FILE IN
THE HAWAII STATE DEPARTMENT OF HEALTH

Alvin T. Onaka, Ph.D.

STATE REGISTRAR

64 – The Stamp Shows Several Signs It's Not in the Best Condition

As with a number of our other theories so far, this one also completely fails the common sense test.

We know that the Hawaii Department of Health claims to have certified and sent the birth certificate. We even have a signed letter from none other than the Director of the Hawaii State Department of Health, Loretta J. Fuddy, attesting to the fact. And we also have an official statement on the Hawaii Department of Health web site.

Now if the Hawaii Department of Health went to all this trouble to certify a birth certificate for Barack Obama (whether it is legitimate or not) – and remember that they have basically confessed that the document posted is the one they sent – *why wouldn't they also use an official stamp?*

In addition, the "Alvin T. Onaka" signature, and the stamp in general, match other published photographs of Mr. Onaka's stamp.

Why would anyone, *particularly* the Hawaii Department of Health (which has at least one and probably several legitimate Alvin T. Onaka stamps), *forge* a stamp and get Mr. Onaka's signature absolutely correct, but completely miss the fact that they had misspelled the word "THE?"

The theory simply makes no sense. And the fact that Dr. Jerome Corsi has made such a weak claim is disturbing.

But as we will see, it's going to get even worse.

DID THE FORGER LEAVE
A SMILEY FACE?

"With a magnification of 800 percent, the distinct form of a smiley face can be seen on the side of the 'A' in Onaka's first name. The figure appears to be a side profile of a face with a nose, eye and mouth." [108]

– Dr. Jerome Corsi, WorldNetDaily Article

This is rather like the famous "face on Mars."

In 1976, NASA's Viking 1 spacecraft snapped a photo of what looked very much like a human face in the middle of a lot of other (less interesting) rocky features on the red planet.

For many years, the Martian face was a staple of supermarket tabloids.

By 2001, however, we had gained a much better view of the mesa that the Viking spacecraft had photographed from orbit. [109]

As you can see, there's a little bit of resemblance to a human face even in the 2001 photo. But the later photo makes clear that the resemblance is only a superficial one, and that most of the "Martian face" is in the *perception* of the beholder.

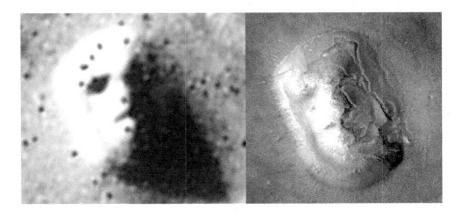

65 – By 2001, The Famous Face on Mars Was Unmasked as Just A Mesa

As human beings, our minds are designed to try and make sense of complex graphic information. The same marvelous brain that lets us peer through a tangled mess of forest branches and leaves and discern the face of another human being – based upon a mere glimpse – also lets us envision a face on a Martian mesa when enough graphic cues are there to allow us to construct one.

It's the same thing here. When you look at the "A" in the signature stamp from the green background document, it's easy to construct a smiling cartoon face in profile.

A close look at the AP image again reveals what we saw in the last chapter: There are gaps and smudges in the stamp.

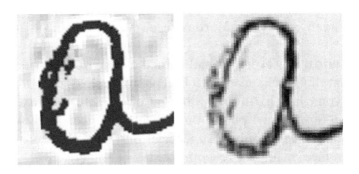

66 – The "Smiley Face" of Obama's Certificate Unmasked

DID THE FORGER LEAVE HIS INITIALS IN THE BIRTH CERTIFICATE?

" The 'THE' is a 'TXE' or a 'TKE,' it's not a 'THE...' Now that smiley face is formed with an 'E' that is written into the loop of the 'A.' So you got the last two letters there of 'KE.'

And I can also show you in that document where you can find the 'MI.' So 'MIKE' is written into this document. I'm pretty confident 'Mike' is the first name of the guy who forged it." [110]

– Dr. Jerome Corsi, on the Tom Tancredo Show

In spite of Dr. Corsi's confidence, there is simply no real evidence to support this claim.

He has already claimed that the "H" in "THE" is an "X." Having done that, he now *changes his mind* and claims it's a "K."

But why a "K"? We certainly don't get there by actually looking at the letter.

The obvious reason is that if it's a "K" instead of an "X," then he might be able to construct "MIKE."

Aha! The name of a forger.

But it isn't a "K." It isn't even an "X." It's just a smudged and deteriorated "H."

If it were a "K," we wouldn't have the big indentation in the left side of the letter. It would be straight. We wouldn't have the faint straight edge on the right-hand side of the letter, either. (Unless it's a *backwards* "K?" That might work.)

And the supposed "E," obviously, is simply another case where the mind can construct a letter where one really doesn't exist – just like the "face on Mars" phenomenon.

A reference back to the more nuanced, grayscaled views of the "H" in "THE" and the "A" in "Alvin," – as shown in the past two chapters – are really all that is needed to illustrate the absurdity of this particular claim.

67 – Now All We Need Is the "MI" ?

OTHER ISSUES

There are a few other issues we should deal with, briefly, in regard to the *information* on the birth certificate.

Is The Hospital Name Wrong?

Shortly after the certificate was released, it was reported by some that the hospital was not called the "Kapiolani Maternity & Gynecological Hospital" back in 1961.

This rumor has widely been shown to be false. And in fact, the exact same name appears on the birth certificates of the Nordyke twins.[111]

It turns out that the hospital name is correct.

A Different Doctor Was Reported Earlier

Some sources (including *snopes.com*) reported before the release that the delivering doctor was a Dr. Rodney T. West.[112] This conflicts with the information on the certificate that Obama was delivered by Dr. David Sinclair.

The statement was based on a claim from Barbara Nelson, Obama's high school English teacher. Mrs. Nelson, in an interview, stated, "I may be the only person left who specifically remembers [Barack Obama's] birth."

She recounts a conversation with a Dr. Rodney West at dinner one day in Hawaii. She asked the obstetrician to tell her something interesting that had happened that week. Dr. West reportedly replied, "Well, today, Stanley had a baby." [113]

The assumption that Dr. West was actually the delivering doctor is based on a conversation that happened nearly 50 years before, concerning a baby that Ms. Nelson did not yet personally know at the time. The enormous time gap alone makes for questionable reliability.

And Dr. West may very well have been recounting a story from something that happened "at work" that he personally was not involved in. The fact that a half African baby was born to a young woman named Stanley would likely have been an interesting topic of conversation.

In fact, since Ms. Nelson claims to have heard firsthand about Obama's birth, *in Hawaii*, the story actually *supports* a Hawaiian birth for Barack Obama.

Does Kapiolani Hospital Hold Admission Records for Stanley Ann Dunham Obama?

The short answer is, we don't know, and probably can't.

Dr. Jerome Corsi has claimed, "Kapiolani, by the way, even today, even after this long form birth certificate has been released, still has provided no patient records of Ann Dunham. In fact, I've interviewed people who just won't go on the record, in Hawaii, who sit in the quarterly meetings of the hospital administrators, that they've been holding for a long time in Hawaii, and since 2008 the hospital administrators in Hawaii have been looking for birth records of Obama or Ann Dunham as a patient, and none of them have those records. You'll never see them." [114]

At this point, the claim is based entirely upon the word of Dr. Jerome Corsi, quoting anonymous sources who "won't go on the record." And as we've seen, Dr. Corsi has been less than a reliable source of completely accurate information in regard to certain other aspects of the birth certificate issue.

It's understandable, of course, that any anonymous sources would not wish to have their names revealed publicly. Hospitals and their employees are *legally prohibited* from disclosing any patient information, except to actual patients or their personal representatives, or to the US Department of Health and Human Services in the course of an official investigation.

Here's the rule:

"A covered entity must disclose protected health information in only two situations: (a) to individuals (or their personal representatives) specifically when they request access to, or an accounting of disclosures of, their protected health information; and (b) to HHS when it is undertaking a compliance investigation or review or enforcement action." [115]

Disclosure of patient information is a *crime*. The penalties for this are not small, and would apply to the person soliciting and *receiving* the information as well as to the person disclosing it:

"A person who knowingly obtains or discloses individually identifiable health information in violation of the Privacy Rule may face a criminal penalty of up to $50,000 and up to one-year imprisonment. The criminal penalties increase to $100,000 and up to five years imprisonment if the wrongful conduct involves false pretenses, and to $250,000 and up to 10 years imprisonment if the wrongful conduct involves the intent to sell, transfer, or use identifiable health information for commercial advantage, personal gain or malicious harm." [116]

Claims that Kapiolani Hospital has no records for Stanley Ann Dunham Obama are therefore not only unsubstantiated, but are based on information that would be *highly* illegal for any hospital employee to disclose, even anonymously.

Does Barack Obama, Sr.'s Race Indicate Fraud?

The claim here is that in 1961, the official racial designation for an African-American would have been "Negro," and that the use of the word "African" is a "smoking gun" that indicates the birth certificate information was only very recently compiled.

This theory looks like it was resolved in August 2008. At that time, one Jessica Henig (working for *FactCheck.org*), wrote:

"We received responses to some of our questions from the Hawaii Department of Health. They couldn't tell us anything about their security paper, but they did answer another frequently raised question: why is Obama's father's race listed as 'African'?"

"Kurt Tsue at the DOH told us that father's race and mother's race are supplied by the parents, and that 'we accept what the parents self identify themselves to be.'" [117]

FactCheck.org is regarded by many conservatives as being highly biased in favor of Mr. Obama. And that may well be. However, they do name a clear source for the information.

According to an official Department of Health news release posted on the web site of the state of Hawaii, as of January 2011, there was indeed a Kurt Tsue working for the Hawaii Department of Health. [118]

So according to the Department of Health, if Stanley Ann Dunham Obama said the father was "African," then "African" it was. And it's very easy to imagine that a young white woman in 1961 might have preferred to have the race of her child's father listed as "African" rather than "Negro."

Not only that, but we know from the 1955 article by Bennett and Tokuyama (introduced by Dr. Corsi on the topic of the certificate number), that the person originally filling out the form would *not* have been a Department of Health official, but a clerk or nurse at the hospital. [119]

Changing the race to anything different from what was submitted would have therefore required extra work in the form of going back and consulting with the hospital and the mother, who by that time would have been dismissed and sent home.

Human beings, even government officials, don't normally like doing a significant amount of additional work for the purpose of changing an unimportant point. Far better to stamp the document and file it.

Barack Obama, Sr.'s Age Incorrect?

The reported age for Barack Obama Sr. is 25.[120] However, Barack Obama Sr.'s immigration file indicates that he was actually 27 at the time.[121]

Stanley Ann Dunham Obama is listed on the birth certificate as the person supplying the information. And she most likely would've put whatever Barack Obama Sr. had told her.

Jerome Corsi, however (supporting the theory of a birth in Kenya), writes, "The discrepancy in Obama Sr.'s reported age might be explained if the grandparents appeared alone at the Hawaii DOH office in Honolulu to report the birth, without Barack Obama Sr. or Ann Dunham appearing with them." [122]

Mr. Obama is reported to have been a "slippery character" who was investigated by US Customs and Immigrations officials on suspicion of polygamy.[123] And by all accounts, he and Stanley Ann Dunham were not married when she became pregnant at the age of 17.[124]

It's easy to see why Mr. Obama might have wanted to minimize his age. Some things are a bit easier to get away with when you are young and immature. Impregnating a 17-year-old girl is a lot harder to get away with when you start to be perceived as pushing 30.

What Was Kenya Called in 1961?

Some have claimed that the use of the word "Kenya" on the birth certificate indicates that it's a fraud, since Kenya didn't become independent of the United Kingdom until 1963 – two years after Barack Obama was born. The claim is that "British East Africa" would have been used instead.

It is not difficult to find out what Kenya might have been commonly called in 1961. All one has to do is to look up a map from the period. It's easy, for example, to find a 1960 National Geographic map of the world online.[125]

On the 1960 map, Kenya is part of a larger colonial territory labeled, in different places, "U.K." and "Tr. Terr. U.K."

Several large areas are part of this huge territory. These are labeled "UGANDA," "KENYA," "RUANDA," "TANGANYIKA," "ZANZIBAR," and so forth.

The last two of these were later combined into a single entity, so these territories are what are known today as the nations of Uganda, Kenya, Rwanda, and Tanzania.

The interesting thing is that the name "Kenya" appears on the National Geographic 1960 map... but the words "British East Africa" do not.

The actual birthplace of Barack Obama's father listed on the long-form birth certificate is "Kenya, East Africa." So in fact, both names are covered.

Was The Registrar Really Called "Ukulele?"

A few people have claimed that the name of the registrar, which appears to be "UKL Lee," is some kind of forger's joke; and that the birth certificate is therefore a flagrant fraud.

This registrar is known to have existed, as the same signature (which is visible in our first illustration, on page 2) appeared on the birth certificate of Edith Pauline Coats in June of 1962.[126]

And the owner of the signature now appears to have been identified. It seems that the "U" is actually a "V," and the signature is that of Verna K. L. Lee, who was listed in a 1961 city directory as an employee with the Department of Health.[127]

Relevant Happenings

In this chapter, we will look briefly at a few issues *outside of the document itself* that might have some bearing on it.

Was Barack Obama Adopted in Indonesia?

There has been speculation that Barack Obama was adopted as a child by Lolo Soetoro, his Indonesian stepfather. *WorldNetDaily* cites evidence that a registration card for an Indonesian school listed Obama (under the name "Barry Soetoro") as an Indonesian citizen.[128]

Unless he was formally adopted in the United States, or US papers were filed registering the adoption, we would not expect his Hawaiian birth certificate to show adoption amendments.

I am not a lawyer (nor do I play one on TV), but at this point, based on the reading I've done, it seems to me that United States law is fairly clear: Assuming that Mr. Obama was born a US citizen, no act on the part of his parents could have deprived him of that citizenship.[129]

Another issue is that Obama was born a dual citizen of the US and the UK. This fact appears to have been acknowledged by the Obama campaign in the last election.[130]

There's a lot that can be said about this issue. That, however, is beyond the scope of this book. All we are trying to answer here is whether or not we have credible evidence that the long-form birth certificate is a forgery.[131]

Did Barack Obama Pay $2 Million on Lawyers in Order to Avoid Releasing His Long-Form Birth Certificate?

Barack Obama's campaign has reportedly spent at least $2.8 million in legal fees following the 2008 presidential election.[132]

However, campaigns incur large legal fees, and the size and finances of the 2008 Obama campaign were a record-breaking $778 million. The McCain campaign, which raised about half as much, reportedly paid more than $1.3 million in legal fees.[133]

No figure is publicly available on what part of the $2.8 million spent by the Obama campaign on legal assistance has gone specifically to pay attorneys in Obama's eligibility lawsuits.

Literally dozens of such lawsuits have been filed regarding Mr. Obama's presidential eligibility.

However, his personal lawyers have apparently participated in only three. Those cases are *Berg v. Obama, Hollister v. Soetoro,* and *Keyes v. Bowen.*[134]

It is clear that Obama's lawyers have filed, at a minimum, several dozen pages of legal papers on his behalf in these cases. But none of the three cases ever came to trial.[135]

Whatever the amount paid by Mr. Obama to his lawyers for his defense, then, it doesn't appear to be anywhere approaching the amounts that have sometimes been claimed.

In addition, *none* of the three cases would likely have been resolvable just by producing the long-form birth certificate. There are other challenges in them.

All three, for example, allege that Obama became an Indonesian citizen and would thereby have lost his status as a United States natural born citizen.[136] And other parties besides Mr. Obama were involved in *Keyes v. Bowen.*

Legally speaking, producing the long-form birth certificate would probably have been of very little benefit as regards the few court cases that Obama's lawyers were involved in.

An Official from Hawaii Testified that There Was No Birth Certificate.

The official in question is Timothy Adams, who served as a senior elections clerk in Honolulu for roughly four months during the 2008 election.

Mr. Adams has been featured in several *WorldNetDaily* articles, first for making the claim, in June 2010,[137] and then for signing a statement to that effect, the following January.

Adams states in his affidavit, "Senior officers in the City and County of Honolulu Elections Division told me on multiple occasions that no Hawaii long-form, hospital-generated birth certificate existed for Senator Obama in the Hawaii Department of Health and there was no record that any such document had ever been on file in the Hawaii Department of Health or any other branch or department of the Hawaii government."

He also states, "...it was common knowledge among my fellow employees that no Hawaii long-form, hospital-generated birth certificate existed for Senator Obama." [138]

Adams also says, "During the course of my employment, I became aware that many requests were being made to the City and County of Honolulu Elections Division, the Hawaii Office of Elections, and the Hawaii Department of Health from around the country to obtain a copy of then-Senator Barack Obama's long-form, hospital-generated birth certificate."

However, Glen Takahashi, the elections administrator for the city and county of Honolulu, stated to David Weigel (writing for the Washington Post), "Our office does not have access to birth records. That's handled by the state of Hawaii Department of Health... I fielded no questions about that. Why would anyone ask us? We don't have those records." [139]

Mr. Adams has never revealed exactly who the "senior officers" are that he refers to, although he does make it clear that one primary source was a female supervisor.

Taking Mr. Adams at his word and assuming that he's telling the truth, all we have is still just rumors from anonymous sources who were obviously not themselves in a position to know, quoting still *other* anonymous sources who might or might not have been in a position to know. It is, as one writer characterized it, "double hearsay." [140]

This can be compared with clear statements from public officials that Barack Obama was indeed born in the State. These include Republican Governor Linda Lingle, Dr. Chiyome Fukino who served as Director of the Hawaii State Department of Health under her, present Governor Neil Abercrombie, the present Department of Health Director Loretta J. Fuddy, and Registrar Alvin T. Onaka, whose signature stamp appears on the Obama birth certificate.

Republican Governor Linda Lingle stated in May of 2010, "I had my Health Director, who is a physician by background, go personally view the birth certificate in the birth records of the Department of Health, and we issued a news release at that time saying that the president was, in fact, born at Kapiolani Hospital in Honolulu, Hawaii." [141]

Dr. Chiyome Fukino, Health Director under Governor Lingle, has repeatedly confirmed Obama's birth in Hawaii. One example is this statement from October 2008, "I, as Director of Health for the State of Hawai'i, along with the Registrar of Vital Statistics... [Alvin T. Onaka, whose certifying signature stamp appears on the Obama certificate], have personally seen and verified that the Hawai'i State Department of Health has Senator Obama's original birth certificate on record in accordance with state policies and procedures." [142]

Hawaii Governor Neil Abercrombie has stated, "Considering all of the investigations that have been done and the information that has been provided, no rational person can question the President's citizenship. We have found a way – once again – to confirm what we already knew: the President was born here in Hawai'i. State officials of both parties have verified that President Obama's birth records show that he was born in Honolulu." [143]

Health Director Loretta J. Fuddy also stated in April 2011, "We hope that issuing certified copies of the original Certificate of Live Birth to President Obama will end the numerous inquiries related to his birth in Hawai'i. I have seen the original records filed at the Department of Health and attest to the authenticity of the certified copies the department provided to the President that further prove the fact that he was born in Hawai'i." [144]

As for Alvin Onaka, his stamp appears on the document itself, and he has made no statement to the contrary. So I would say that constitutes an official statement as well.

Did the Governor of Hawaii State That No Birth Certificate Existed?

On January 20, 2011, a radio personality named Mike Evans claimed on the radio that he had been told by Hawaii Governor Neil Abercrombie that there was no birth certificate:

"Yesterday talking to Neil's office, Neil says that he searched everywhere using his power as Governor, at the Kapiolani Women's and Children's Hospital and Queens Hospital, the only places kids were born in Hawaii back when Barack was born... *There is no Barack Obama birth certificate in Hawaii... Absolutely no proof at all that he was born in Hawaii.*" [145]

Less than a week later, however, Evans completely changed his tune, telling Fox News, "Only this I can you tell you is 100 percent fact: that Neil never told me there was no birth certificate. I never talked to him." [146]

So did someone "get to" Mike Evans? Or is there another explanation?

Dr. Jerome Corsi certainly seemed to do nothing to dispel the idea that somebody had "gotten to" Evans. On the Peter Boyles radio show on January 26, he stated, "Look, this is typical what goes on with the Barack Obama birth certificate issues. The backtracking and cover-up starts almost immediately, as soon as someone's told the truth." [147]

Evans himself, however, gives an explanation for what happened: On January 18, he had read an online article which stated that Governor Abercrombie couldn't find a birth certificate for Barack Obama, that there was no record of an Obama birth at either Honolulu hospital, and that a former Honolulu elections clerk had stated that neither hospital had a record of the birth. Evans then called the Governor's office to confirm that. The Governor did not answer the call, and had not called him back. [148]

In fact, there *was* such an article published on January 18, 2011, titled, "Hawaii governor can't find Obama birth certificate."

It was written by Jerome Corsi. [149]

It appears, then, that we seem to have a kind of bizarre "feedback loop" –

- On January 17, 2011, the Honolulu Star-Advertiser interviewed Governor Neil Abercrombie, asking him, "You stirred up quite a controversy with your comments regarding birthers and your plans to release more information regarding President Barack Obama's birth certificate. How is that coming?"

- Abercrombie replied regarding the birth certificate, "It was actually written I am told, this is what our investigation is showing, it actually exists in the archives, written down... What I can do, and all I have ever said, is that I am going to see to it as governor that I can verify to anyone who is honest about it that this is the case." [150]

- The following day, January 18, Dr. Jerome Corsi published an article for *WorldNetDaily* titled, "Hawaii governor can't find Obama birth certificate," claiming, "Hawaii Gov. Neil Abercrombie suggested in an interview published today that a long-form, hospital-generated birth certificate for Barack Obama may not exist within the vital records maintained by the Hawaii Department of Health." (This would appear, by the way, to be a mischaracterization of what Abercrombie actually said.)

- Mike Evans then read Corsi's article, called the Governor's office on the 19th, and failed to speak to Governor Abercrombie.

- The following morning, January 20, Evans got onto the radio and repeated Corsi's interpretation of Abercrombie's words, mixed with Corsi's and Adams' claims that no birth certificate existed – and attributed it all to the Governor.

- The news began to break far and wide: *Hawaii Governor Neil Abercrombie has admitted to his old friend Mike Evans that Barack Obama's birth certificate does not exist!*

- Six days later, Mike Evans had to publicly retract his attribution of Corsi's and Adams' words to Governor Neil Abercrombie – and Corsi claimed that Evans was now backtracking after having spoken the truth.

The Strange Certification by Nancy Pelosi

In September of 2009, J.B. Williams, reporting for the *Canada Free Press*, broke the news that the Democrat Party had prepared two different certification letters regarding their Presidential and Vice-Presidential candidates.

The article included notarized copies of both letters, which were signed by Nancy Pelosi (acting as Chair of the Democratic National Convention), and Alice Travis Germond, Secretary of the Democratic National Convention.

One letter read:

"THIS IS TO CERTIFY that at the National Convention of the Democrat Party of the United States of America, held in Denver, Colorado on August 25 though 28, 2008, the following were duly nominated as candidates of said Party for President and Vice President of the United States respectively and that the following candidates for President and Vice President of the United States are legally qualified to serve under the provisions of the United States Constitution."

The second letter read:

"THIS IS TO CERTIFY that at the National Convention of the Democrat Party of the United States of America, held in Denver, Colorado on August 25 though 28, 2008, the following were duly nominated as candidates of said Party for President and Vice President of the United States respectively." [151]

Notice what's missing?

The second letter – the one *without* the language specifying that the candidates were legally qualified to serve under the Constitution of the United States – is the one that was sent by the Democrat Party to most States to certify their candidates to those States.

In fact, J.B. Williams initially believed that the letter without the eligibility language was sent to all 50 States. This turned out not to be the case, however. Mr. Williams corrected his initial assumption in a follow-up article 5 days later which acknowledged that the "long form" (as he termed it) had been filed at least with the State of Hawaii. [152]

The creation and filing of a letter that specifically leaves out certification of eligibility seems very suspicious. Why on earth would the Democrat Party do this, unless some real doubt existed about whether at least one of their candidates was Constitutionally eligible to serve?

And contrasted with the practice of the Republicans, it looks all the *more* suspicious. As Williams wrote: "[T]hroughout the years and states investigated thus far, the RNC has not failed to certify their candidates as nominees who meet all legal constitutional requirements even once." [153]

For this reason, Mr. Williams presented the theory that Nancy Pelosi and Alice Travis Germond knowingly lied on the letter which states certification of eligibility.

However, Williams later admits in a follow-up article, "Both documents had been used before by the DNC, in 2000 and 2004."

And again, further down: "Now, to be fair, the DNC had been omitting that language from their official filings for years. Refusing to certify their candidates as 'constitutionally eligible' has been a practice of the DNC for at least a few election cycles now. Why?" [154]

This admission is critical, because it demonstrates that at least since 2000, the same practice has consistently been used by the Democrat Party.

Barack Obama first rose to national prominence as keynote speaker at the 2004 Democratic National Convention, while he was still a State Senator. [155]

It is clear, then, that the Democrat Party has been creating two different certification letters – one with, and one without, the language certifying Constitutional eligibility – since years before Barack Obama burst onto the national political scene. They appear to have done nothing different in 2008 than they did in 2000 and 2004, and perhaps for much longer than that.

The practice is certainly (in my opinion) a strange and suspicion-arousing one. I would suspect that they may change it in 2012. They certainly ought to.

But in the meantime, the fact that they've been doing it this way for years means that it can't be considered evidence that Ms. Pelosi or Ms. Germond chose to omit the eligibility language because of doubts about Barack Obama.

By the way, kudos to J.B. Williams for reporting all of the known details, even in the midst of his own suspicions, which obviously remained even after discovering the DNC's past practices. A writer with less integrity might well have left those details out.

––––––––––––––––

We will now turn our attention to three final areas of investigation which I undertook independently, none of which (at the time I undertook them, at least) seemed to have been covered by anybody else.

FINAL AREAS OF
INVESTIGATION

A MYSTERIOUS ANOMALY
IN THE SPACING

Very late one night, I was closely examining the birth certificate.

Having eliminated many different claims of proof of forgery, I had turned my attention to the document's typing.

Around 2 am, I made a strange discovery concerning the alignment of some of the letters on the form.

I realized that the trend I was looking at could easily mean – *if it held at certain other points in the document* – that I had actually *found* the kind of credible proof of forgery that so many people were searching for.

I stopped, sat back, and considered the implications.

A forged birth certificate of a sitting President, whose eligibility had been in public doubt.

A press conference presenting credible proof.

A first small news article, with agencies very reluctant to report at first. Then, the beginnings of public shock as attempts to refute the claim failed. Recognition dawning.

And the beginning of a growing public storm that could most likely only end with the resignation or removal from office of the President of the United States.

The history of a nation changed – forever.

Heart pounding, I turned my attention to the few critical areas of the document that would shortly tell the tale.

The Anomaly

What I had discovered was a misalignment between most of the information on the second line (which could pertain to any baby boy born on any August 4th), and other information – which was clearly specific to Barack Obama.

This meant that the two "blocks" of information had *not* been entered all as one smooth unit. At a minimum, the paper had been shifted by the typist in between entering the two blocks of info. At a maximum, they were entered at two different times, *and by two completely different people.*

An obvious theory, then, was that the certificate was forged – built on top of some other child's birth certificate, with original information erased and the info for Barack Obama filled in.

If so, some other pieces of information might be left over from the original form. And a clear misalignment between the original information and what was added had the potential to pretty well *prove* that tampering had taken place.

The specific information in misalignment – both vertical and horizontal – was most of the information in the second line: the gender of the child ("Male"), the "X" designating a single birth, and the date ("August 4") *up to but not including the comma or the "1961."*

68 – *An Anomaly: Most of the Information in the Second Line is Misaligned*

Although the lines I drew aren't 100% perfect, in the illustration you can clearly see that the word "August" and the numeral "4" are not left-to-right aligned with the rest of the text.

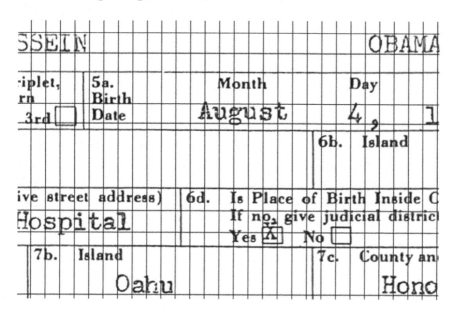

69 – A Closer View of the Misalignment

Consulting the "1" to the right of the "4" also reveals the *vertical* misalignment: "August" and "4" are *higher* than the other characters on the same line.

This is less evident with the "4," since its bottom stroke tends to go below the line (this can be seen in its next occurrence). However, it is still visible even in that case when you compare the top of the "4" against the top of the "1."

Two competing theories were possible: Either the misaligned information had come from an original certificate used as the basis for a forgery, or the typist had simply typed that bit of information separately from the other info – either removing the form completely from the typewriter, or hitting the paper release and repositioning it before continuing.

But which theory was the right one?

On Three X's Hang the Fate of the Nation

The forgery theory meant that someone might have erased and replaced only the relevant, Obama-specific areas of the form.

And there was a way to at least partially test for the theory.

If some other area of the form contained general information that ought to apply to anybody, and *if* that information were aligned with the gender, single birth and date information – and if it were *not* aligned with the Obama-specific information – then we would almost certainly have credible evidence of a forgery.

Why? Because a typist might realign or refeed the paper before typing a particular line, but would *never* have skipped through typing only selected information, and then gone back through and typed in all of the child-specific info.

And the form does contain other general information of this kind.

The information of interest consists of the X's in the check boxes that serve as answers to the following questions:

- "Is Place of Birth Inside City or Town Limits?"
- "Is Residence Inside City or Town Limits?"
- "Is Resident on a Farm or Plantation?"

A close examination (referring back to Illustration 68) shows that the X's in these three boxes are aligned *not* with the gender/single birth/month/day information, but with all the rest of the (Obama-specific) information on the form.

And with that discovery, our potential evidence of forgery began to evaporate.

Digging Deeper

We shouldn't totally let go of the forgery theory just yet, however.

Again, there are two possible theories to explain the origin of the document, and the misalignment.

One theory is that the original, underlying image is exactly what it claims to be: an image of an original paper document, typed by a nurse or clerk at Kapiolani Hospital, and certified by the State of Hawaii.

The other is that the image, from the very beginning, was artificially created.

In order for the latter to be the case, it would almost certainly have been created from pieces of real, original documents.[156]

If we are to choose which of our two theories is the more likely explanation, we need some method that ought to help us get at the truth.

The best approach is likely to be to assume each possibility in turn, and then see whether what we see on the document makes sense and can be explained by our assumptions.

Considering the Forgery Theory

Let us assume, then, that someone has forged the document, and let us ask why we see the characters aligned exactly as they are.

We know that all of the information *except for* the partial line giving gender, single birth, and "August 4" (but *not* the comma that follows), was entered at one time, as a single block of information... Or at least, it very much appears to have been.

If this information was *not* done as a single block, then it has been very, *very* carefully aligned.

Therefore, if someone has forged the document, they were very careless with the alignment of the misaligned (gender/ single birth/ August 4) block of information.

Or, things were done deliberately in this way, in order to produce a "red herring."

Such a red herring would probably be of no value, however. As with other anomalies regarding the document, *not* having this misalignment would arouse much less suspicion than having it.

The only conclusion we can reasonably come to, then, is that the misalignment does not particularly serve the purposes of a forger. If it is there (and it is), it would have to be a mark of extreme carelessness on the part of an otherwise very careful and professional forger.

Since this is fairly unlikely, as long as there is a plausible explanation for the phenomenon *outside of* forgery, the misalignment probably is not an indicator that the document is a fake.

But *is* there another plausible explanation?

Considering the Authenticity Theory

Having assumed forgery – and not gotten anywhere in particular with the assumption – let us now assume that the document is genuine.

Is there then a reasonable explanation for the misalignment?

If it's genuine, then the nurse or clerk typing it must have either completely removed the sheet of paper and reinserted it, or released the paper from the platen and readjusted it.

We have two blocks of information: the small block containing only the gender/single birth/month/day information, and the larger block of information containing everything else.

Which came first?

Solving the "Which Came First?" Puzzle

A little thought will make clear which of the two blocks of information must have been typed first.

It is much more common, and far more likely, to *break off* typing in the middle of a line, than it is to *begin* typing right in the middle of a line.

We have, however, an even better indicator than that.

The comma.

If a typist were to begin by typing the year (1961), leaving off the day and month to be filled in later (August 4), he or she would almost certainly begin with the year itself, *and not with the comma that precedes the year.* As a rule, *no one* ever just starts typing with a comma.

But the comma is aligned with the year that follows it, and *not* with the month and day that precede it.

Month	Day	Year	5b. Hour /
August	4 ,	1961	7:24 P.M.
	6b. Island		
	Oahu		

70 – The Comma Is Aligned with Year and Time of Birth

The best assumption, then, is that the comma and year, typed together, were *filled in* as a follow-up to information already on the document.

So while we can't know with absolute, 100% assurance, we can come close. The *first* information typed was *almost certainly* the gender/ single birth/ month/ day information.

Two Theories as to Why

Two reasonable theories come to mind as explanations for why this may have happened.

The first is that a nurse or clerk knew that a boy had been born, but didn't yet know the name, so he or she went ahead and typed the information indicating the birth of a non-twin male on August 4.

The second theory (and the one I think more likely) is that the information was reported verbally, perhaps by a nurse to a clerk or typist, and there was some uncertainty regarding the spelling or some other aspect of the baby's name – so the typist began with the second line instead of the first.

In fact, the uncertainty could have been in the mind of Stanley Ann Dunham Obama. Was she really sure that she wanted to name her son Barack? Was she sure about the middle name? Was she certain that she wanted him to be a "Junior" to a man with whom she faced an uncertain future? Did she want the name to be the very foreign-sounding "Barack," or "Barry?"

She may have taken a minute to fully make up her mind, and the nurse or clerk typed some of the information that *was* available while waiting.

Then, the decision made – or the clarification as to spelling finally reached – the typist released the paper from the platen, readjusted it at the beginning of the form, and finished typing all the rest of the details.

CERTIFICATE NUMBERS COMPARED

Having found that the misalignment was explainable by legitimate means, I then asked what other unexplored items might potentially provide proof of a forgery.

Others have compared the birth certificate number to that of known birth certificates, such as those of the Nordyke twins. Let's compare the physical appearance of the number stamp itself.

71 – Overlay of Certificate Number Stamps

The image we have for the Nordyke twins is much lower resolution, but it will still prove very useful. In the illustration, I've overlaid the certificate number from Susan Nordyke's birth certificate with that of Barack Obama's.

It is clear that each individual number appears to be in exactly the same place on both certificates – just as we would expect them to be if the same stamp had been used, only a few documents apart.

And the numbers are in very characteristic places. They "travel" up and down. Yet each corresponding numeral is in the exact right place for both documents to have been stamped with the same stamp.

When you scale the certificate numbers to match in size, the words on the form appear to be the exact same size as well.

DOES THE FORM MATCH?

Our investigation of the birth certificate is nearly complete. Only one item, as far as I know or can think of, remains.

Like the comparison of the certificate number stamps, this is also something that no one else besides myself, as far as I can tell, has yet written about.

It is still possible, even at this very late date, that we might yet uncover a discrepancy that would lead to the discovery of a fraud.

If the Obama birth certificate is authentic, then the *form* ought to match that which is seen in other birth certificates of the day.

If there is any significant deviation in the actual form itself, then that would lead us to suspect a fraud.

An overlay of the AP and Nordyke documents (on the following page, and this time I chose Gretchen's, as it has a bit more margin at the left) shows that again, taking into account a small amount of distortion caused by different camera angles – the forms apparently *do* match.

The curve appears to be slightly less on the Nordyke certificate than on the Obama one. This is easily explained by there having been a slightly different camera angle.

So the form itself appears to be the same. Every element is the same size and proportion; and every element is in the same place.

72 – The Nordyke and Obama Forms Match

At this point, we have pretty well reached the limits of what we can determine without a hands-on examination of the physical, paper documents.

We are now ready to take a look at how well our experts have done, wrap up a few final issues, and come to our conclusions about the birth certificate's authenticity.

How Do the Experts Score?

Earlier we listed ten people who have been named as experts or influential voices regarding the Obama birth certificate.

Six of those have spoken in favor of a forgery, three have spoken against evidence for forgery, and one has seemed fairly neutral on the question.

So why do the "for's," at this point, outnumber the "against's?"

Part of the answer is that a few of the individuals in the "for" group have experience and points of view that may not be adequate for, or not quite applicable to, the task. One is a teenager; one is mostly a business owner; another is mostly a financial specialist; one is a writer of non-technical books. Another is a typographer working with distorted fonts.

Another factor might be that there has been a eager audience ready to provide some degree of instant fame to individuals who are prepared to come out on the side of forgery.[157] As I myself discovered when I posted my first videos to YouTube, a careful, reasoned evaluation just didn't seem to have the same "legs" as a far less careful claim of an "absolute proof" that the document was forged.

And it's very easy to allege forgery. All you have to do is to find something odd about the document, and then claim that the oddity "proves" a fraud.

I have heard people ask, "Well, if the birth certificate *isn't* a fake, then why is it that not one single expert has come forward to state that it's authentic?"

Well, the best experts are very *careful* about the claims they make.

A claim of authenticity is a big claim, and it requires a great deal of authoritative knowledge to "prove" that a document is authentic.

In fact, one of the things that it probably pretty well requires is somehow demonstrating that *no* claim to the contrary is credible. In the case of a large number of claims, this takes an enormous amount of evaluation and work.

But even if a lack of credible forgery claims is successfully demonstrated, it can still be extremely difficult for the honest and careful evaluator to truly guarantee that a document is "authentic." As we noted earlier, a document might pass every single test, and still be a very expertly-produced fake.

In my personal view, a *good* expert should not attempt to state authoritatively that a document "is authentic" without – at a minimum – full access to the original document; and in this case, the record-keeping systems.

This is something we do not have.

Since we don't have such access, then, we are limited to forming an *opinion,* based on the evidence we *do* have.

This includes our detailed, point-by-point analysis, and it includes the relevant statements from the Hawaii Department of Health testifying as to the document's authenticity. On these things we must base our conclusions.

Returning now to the main topic of this chapter – how did our experts do?

Dr. Jerome Corsi

Dr. Jerome Corsi appears to be the authority hardest hit by our careful examination of the facts.

Dr. Corsi has publicly promoted, either in writing or on the radio, at least *twenty-three* evidence-of-fraud theories that we cover in this book.

In writing and speaking about his own theories as well as those of others, he has publicly identified the following as potential indicators of fraud:

- the nature of the layers[158]
- alleged editing of items on the certificate
- the white halo[159]
- the duplicated characters[160]
- the date stamps[161]
- the "scanner with x-ray vision"
- the altered PDF posted at archiveindex.com by Doug Vogt
- the supposed kerning[162]
- comparison with the "African birth" forgery
- the supposed lack of text curvature[163]
- the apparent lack of a seal
- the alignment of Ann Dunham Obama's signature[164]
- the supposed existence of "hidden text"
- the idea that a different document exists[165]
- the out-of-sequence birth certificate number
- Paul Irey's theory of different typefaces
- the supposed misspelling of the word "THE"
- the supposed "smiley face" in the signature stamp
- the supposed record of the forger's initials
- the supposed lack of hospital records for Mrs. Obama
- the discrepancy in Barack Obama, Sr.'s age
- the allegations by Tim Adams[166]
- and the idea that Governor Abercrombie had stated that no birth certificate existed.

As we have seen, *not a single one* of these twenty-three alleged indicators or "proofs" that the document is a fraud or invalid really holds up under close examination.

Not one.

And Corsi has not exactly been restrained in his comments, predicting, "This is going to make Watergate look like a political sideshow by comparison." [167]

It goes without saying that 0 out of 23 isn't a very good record.

Karl Denninger

Karl Denninger has argued that blurring in the form area, a lack of chromatic aberration, kerning, a lack of text curvature, and the use of tab stops are all evidence suggesting forgery.

Mr. Denninger has come up with some original theories. However, I believe we can now consider each of these to be disproven as proofs of forgery.

Douglas B. Vogt

I found Douglas Vogt's 28-page "Final Affidavit" interesting and informative in its discussion of document imaging systems, and we ought to give him credit for his knowledge in that area.

However, moving beyond the topic of document imaging systems, Mr. Vogt states that the document is a forgery for the following reasons:

1. Curved and non-curved type.
2. The white halo.
3. The separation between "binary" (that is, solid-color) and grayscaled letters.
4. The out-of-sequence certificate number.
5. Different colors in the Registrar date stamp areas.
6. The official seal not being part of the certificate, and being the wrong size.
7. The supposed misspelling of the word "THE," a claim that the stamp is "too straight on the form," and the supposed "E" in the capital "A" of "Alvin."

8. The fact that parts of the signatures by Stanley Ann Dunham and the Registrar are single-color, and parts are grayscaled.
9. The layers and the duplicate characters.

We've dealt with all of these, except for the claim that the date stamp is "too straight."

In regard to that, since it "warps" unevenly on the form, some elements clearly *aren't* straight. And a close examination shows that the "Alvin T. Onaka" signature stamp, in fact, slants slightly upward towards the right.

Having addressed that small item, I believe we can now regard Vogt's "irrefutable proof" – *in all nine of his points* – as clearly refuted.

Albert Renshaw

Albert Renshaw lists the layers, the division between solid-color and grayscaled items, scaling, and rotation of elements as proofs of forgery.

As we've seen, none of these is the case.

Earlier, we quoted Albert as saying, "This is clearly a fake. There's no doubt about it, and it's pretty poorly done, too."

However, to his credit, when asked on July 31 whether he had any doubts as to whether the document was a forgery, he replied, "Well, yeah, there's a lot of doubts that it's fraudulent." [168]

I have a daughter who is a similar age to Mr. Renshaw. I wish him a successful career and life in college and beyond.

Alex Jones

As a media personality, Jones is merely repeating the claims of others, although in my opinion, he seems to add a twist of sensationalism wherever possible.

Those who are interested in following Mr. Jones' radio and internet broadcasts may be interested to know that he is also well-known as a "9/11 Truther." [169]

Ivan Zatkovich

Ivan Zatkovich was hired by *WorldNetDaily* to examine the birth certificate and issue a report.

Mr Zatkovich spent, at most, two days looking at the document, and it was an early and first look. He seems to have done a competent job, making comments where he could and refraining from making claims that he couldn't back up.

While I have not written about Mr. Zatkovich's report in full detail, it was, in my opinion, professionally done.

Dr. Neal Krawetz

Dr. Neal Krawetz promptly examined the PDF file released by the White House, and noted nothing suspicious.

Dr. Krawetz has an impressive grasp of the ins and outs of how PDF files work. My compliments to his expertise in that area.

Nathan Goulding

Compliments are also due to Nathan Goulding for promptly demonstrating that layers were not necessarily a sign of forgery.

The fact that he, as a writer for a major conservative magazine, had no hesitation in doing so is also a sign of his journalistic integrity.

Kevin Davidson

Kevin Davidson goes by the web nickname of "Dr. Conspiracy." He is the proprietor of the *Obama Conspiracy Theories* web site, at *www.obamaconspiracy.org*.

We can note that Mr. Davidson is an Obama supporter. If this unduly biases his site, it doesn't seem to be immediately evident. I certainly haven't read all of the info at his large site. However, I haven't noted anything ill-reasoned or manipulatively argued in what I *have* read.

And the only topic I've seen by Kevin Davidson which I felt he hadn't covered as much as he might have, or managed to effectively and honestly refute, was the issue of two different notarized letters from the Democratic National Convention to certify that party's Presidential and Vice-Presidential candidates for the election.

As we have seen here, though, this way of doing things, however questionable, was put in place long before Mr. Obama came along.

While I personally disagree with his preference for President, my compliments go to Mr. Davidson for the enormous amount of work he has put into creating an informative site. Whether you agree or disagree with Dr. Conspiracy, it would be a mistake to ignore or avoid him on the topic.

Paul Irey

Paul Irey's contribution has been in the area of analyzing the typefaces.

While the conclusion I reach is very much the opposite of his, I think some credit should nonetheless go to Mr. Irey for recognizing this as an important – even critical – area to analyze in order to understand whether or not the birth certificate is genuine.

Unanswered Questions

"No matter how many people attest to the authenticity of that document, the fact is he didn't do it for two years. He did not put it out. And the question is—it rings so loud, I think, it should in everyone's mind: Even if it's true, why didn't you do it? Even if it's accurate, what was the purpose of holding onto it for all this time?" [170]

– Tom Tancredo, the Tom Tancredo Show

This is perhaps the biggest unanswered question.

Assuming that Barack Obama's birth certificate is genuine, why did he delay for two years while doubts grew, before finally requesting and releasing his long-form birth certificate?

And why the brushing-off of those who asked questions?

Did Mr. Obama not think that American citizens who had doubts deserved a clear and definitive answer? Were hundreds of thousands of American citizens who asked to see the long-form certificate not "worth" sending a letter of request to Hawaii?

Personally speaking, I doubt I will ever forget the tone of ridicule addressed in May 2009 to a reporter who asked White House Press Secretary Robert Gibbs why the President, in light of his clear promises of transparency, couldn't respond to a petition by 400,000 Americans asking to see the long-form certificate.[171]

And why would Mr. Obama allow decorated, 17-year Army physician Lieutenant Colonel Terrence Lakin (who refused orders to deploy to Afghanistan because he questioned whether they were given by a Commander-in-Chief with the legal authority to do so, and who states he believed he was doing so in his sworn duty to uphold the Constitution) to be court-martialed, jailed for half a year, and sentenced to be thrown out of the Army and stripped of his military retirement for the rest of his life,[172] when the proof of eligibility that Terry Lakin requested – the long-form birth certificate[173,174] – was available simply by asking?

Did the President and his advisors think that the long-form birth certificate was a "trump card" they could hold on to, and produce later in order to embarrass political opponents?

Did they consider the controversy on this question to be a convenient distraction from some other issue, such as the President's handling of unemployment and the economy?

Or were they simply completely unconcerned about the questions and doubts of a large number of the American people – estimated at 43% of Americans by December 2010[175] – and the future of a decorated Army physician?

REACHING OVERALL CONCLUSIONS

I have presented the evidence in the curious case of Barack Obama's long-form birth certificate, and I will leave it up to you, the reader, to draw your own conclusions.

However, when it comes to drawing such conclusions, there are a few things we ought to note.

Fire, or Dry Ice?

Many people are likely to think to themselves, "Well, where there's smoke, there's got to be fire."

In other words, some will naturally tend to believe that simply because there are so *many* different accusations, and because there may be a few that we have not been able to rule out with absolute certainty, then the total weight of all of the unproven accusations adds up to a likelihood of forgery.

In fact, this is not necessarily true. Having a large number of *unproven* (and apparently unprovable) accusations is not an indicator of guilt.

It does, however, demonstrate that if one comes up with a large enough number of accusations – and three dozen is quite a few – he or she will probably be able to stumble across several that will be hard to totally dismiss.

In fact, if I were to accuse you of a robbery, could you prove conclusively that you had not done it?

There is a reason why our legal system demands proof of guilt – rather than assuming any person accused is guilty, and then requiring proof of innocence.

And what looks like smoke isn't always an indication of fire. It's possible to generate a lot of "smoke" just by putting enough dry ice onto the stage.

A Second Objection

Some will say, "Well, we looked at a lot of stuff. You probably missed something. And you're probably wrong on some of these points."

That's possible, of course. However, our conclusions have generally been clear, and I think well-reasoned.

If you're in doubt about any of the "proofs" of forgery that I feel we've been able to dismiss, then I would suggest that you go back, reread, and think very carefully through those particular items.

On the Other Hand

On the other hand, disproving the various claims of fraud cannot prove that the birth certificate is genuine.

You may recall that at the beginning of this book, I stated that a birth certificate might pass every single test we could throw at it, and still be a forgery.

Is this likely? You will have to judge that for yourself.

However, we ought to note that the variation in typewritten letters, the document's spacing (including the anomaly we noted), the left-to-right positioning of the words (consistent with that in the Nordyke certificates), the very slight curve of the text at the left, and the characteristics of the numbered stamp – every one of which is a subtle indicator – all seem to be consistent with authenticity.

In other words, *if the document is a forgery, then – far from being a sloppy one – it must have been done by an absolute professional with almost flawless attention to subtle detail.*

Approaching the subject from a bit different angle, Stanley Ann Dunham Obama was a rather different and remarkable young woman. Even so, upon reflection, I find it very unlikely that a white young woman of 18 years would travel by herself, in 1961, literally halfway around the world in order to have her first baby alone in East Africa.

For this reason, the circumstances of the mother weigh against the likelihood of a forgery as well.

Also weighing against the idea of a forgery is the fact that any conspiracy would need to involve:

- high officials in Hawaii state government (most likely, stretching across two gubernatorial administrations of both parties)
- lower-level Department of Health staff
- probably at least one official from the White House
- most likely some intelligence agency personnel
- and Barack Obama himself.

As the number of people required for the conspiracy to work goes up, the likelihood of a successful conspiracy goes down.

Nonetheless, I will admit that it's possible to believe that a fraud has been committed.

I can't say, however, that the evidence from the PDF file, the characteristics of and information seen on the documents we have, the evidence from the Hawaii Department of Health, or the evidence regarding relevant happenings and circumstances support such a conclusion.

But I leave it to you to judge for yourself.

WHERE TO FROM HERE?

I understand that some readers may be relieved at what we've discovered during the course of our investigation. And others may be quite disappointed.

To those who might be disappointed, let me simply say: We've done what we could do, and what eligibility skeptics have in fact been asking for. We've taken the questions seriously. And we've followed them as far as we can.

Whether the results should affirm our original beliefs or not, an analysis of this kind is always helpful for our ability to make decisions. If we know where we stand, that helps us realize what direction we ought to go next.

As someone who has closely examined the long-form birth certificate, I now firmly believe that any legal challenges to Barack Obama's eligibility, based on allegations of forgery – unless some new and compelling evidence is produced that we have not yet seen – will not go anywhere at all.

Nor, based upon all of the evidence I've seen, should they.

Some conservatives may lament the fact that I have "let the cat out of the bag."

In other words, there are people who believe that even weak or untrue allegations have the power to damage Mr. Obama politically (perhaps even preventing his reelection), and that for that reason, I should've kept my mouth shut.

I disagree, and for the following reasons.

First, as conservatives, our integrity is our strength. We, more than liberals, like to talk about things like honesty and integrity.

If we let wrongheaded allegations slide simply for the sake of political convenience, then in my opinion, we begin to indulge in compromise of some of the values that we hold dear.

And if we're prepared to correct wrong statements, even when it might be politically inconvenient for us to do so, then we highlight the fact that integrity, for conservatives, is more than just a word.

Secondly, I think our political system is a bit broken, and it ought to somehow be fixed. And a lot of its broken nature is the degree to which inaccuracy and even lies are allowed to participate in and shape our public debates.

True, I understand that much of this is simply human nature. It's just politics, and it's unlikely we will ever be able to totally rid ourselves of it.

Still, the more that we can engage the issues based on the facts rather than on some distortion of them, the better we'll be able to make good decisions – which are required if we want good results.

When we correct wrong and inaccurate statements on our own side of the aisle, we are setting an example, establishing a precedent, and planting a flag – that *honesty and accuracy are still the standard.*

Third, if a controversy has no known merit, it becomes a distraction from the critical issues that face our nation. These include the national debt. They include unemployment and the economy. They include the hugely different conservative and liberal visions for the future of our nation.

Fourth, I believe the eligibility issues hold potential traps for conservatives. For the record, I don't believe that as many votes as some people think hang upon the issue of doubts about Mr. Obama's eligibility. And those who pursue weak arguments too far may well find that those arguments backfire on them.

I am all for declaring Barack Obama ineligible to be President – if he really *is* ineligible.

But if nobody can produce hard, credible evidence that that's the case, then Mr. Obama must be understood to legitimately be occupying the Office of President, and be recognized as the choice – for now, at least – of the American people.

Whether this President is the right choice to lead us into the next critical phase of our nation's history, of course, is a different matter.

Fifth, if I hadn't written this book, somebody else would have.

And if this book, or one like it, is not written by a political conservative, then conservatives can't take credit for holding our own side of the aisle to the truth.

Should we, instead of holding ourselves to the truth, let others be the ones who do so? And then, should we also let them take the credit for it?

I said earlier that our integrity is our strength. And it is. But unless that integrity is openly on display, it can't serve as an advantage for the image of conservatives.

If we are generally people of strong integrity, then this integrity ought to be seen, and people ought to understand that *here* is a valid reason for trusting the important matters of our nation's future into the hands of conservative candidates.

For too long, politicians and others in our society have gotten away with bending, even twisting the truth. Some have freely profited from doing so, and often at the people's expense.

Our nation is at a crossroads in history. The politicians we've elected over the course of many years have badly mismanaged our affairs.

It's my hope that the people of our country will embrace both integrity and intelligence as we confront our challenges, and as we grapple with issues that will determine not only our own futures, but those of our children and our future generations.

ENDNOTES

1   PDF stands for "Portable Document Format." This computer file format was invented by Adobe in 1993, and has long been a standard for documents we would normally see printed: government forms, company brochures, and even this book.

2   Barack Obama official long-form birth certificate, posted by the White House on April 27, 2011, accessed July 7, 2011, http://www.whitehouse.gov/sites/default/files/rss_viewer/birth-certificate-long-form.pdf

3   A good sample of these is available at: http://4.bp.blogspot.com/-ms1Cwq4HKIQ/Tbr_oNVsWkI/AAAAAAAAFUY/nckfmg943WU/s1600/sign_html_m49e27487.jpg

4   These videos are visible at the Springfield Computer Guy YouTube channel, http://www.youtube.com/user/springfieldcompguy.

5   This phrase seems to be most often used in discussion of the issue. But here's an example of its use in an actual article: "Many experts have gone on the record stating that the 'document' is a forgery." ("AP Lawyer Asks Editor: Do You Still Want to Impeach Obama?", The Post & Email, May 23, 2011, accessed July 15, 2011, http://www.thepostemail.com/2011/05/23/the-associated-press-shows-pro-obama-bias-to-the-post-email-inc/)

6   "WorldNetDaily and World Ahead to Partner on WND Books," pcorlaptop.com, accessed July 6, 2011, http://pcorlaptop.com/made/today180236files/forma91398

7   "About Jerome Corsi," Jerome Corsi web site, accessed July 6, 2011, http://www.jeromecorsi.com/about.php

8   "Karl Denninger," Wikipedia, accessed July 6, 2011, http://en.wikipedia.org/wiki/Karl_Denninger

9   Unruh, Bob, "Web expert: Obama certificate falls short in authenticity," WorldNetDaily, May 08, 2011, accessed July 6, 2011, http://www.wnd.com/?pageId=295189

10 "kdenninger's Channel," YouTube, accessed July 6, 2011, http://www.youtube.com/user/kdenninger#p/u

11 Vogt, Douglas B. et al., "Affidavit," accessed July 6, 2011, http://www.scribd.com/fullscreen/55240893

12 Corsi, Jerome R., "Criminal complaint charges Obama birth record 'forged'," WorldNetDaily, May 31, 2011, accessed July 6, 2011, http://www.wnd.com/?pageId=305705

13 Vogt, Douglas B., "Revised and Expanded Affidavit," accessed July 6, 2011, http://www.archiveindex.com/Obama_expanded_affidavit_5-22-2011.pdf

14   Corsi, Jerome R., "Criminal complaint charges Obama birth record 'forged'," WorldNetDaily, May 31, 2011, accessed July 6, 2011, http://www.wnd.com/?pageId=305705

15   Corsi, Jerome R., "Dr. Corsi Reveals First Name of Birth Certificate Forger – 5/26/2011" (interview with Tom Tancredo), 13:37, May 26, 2011, accessed July 7, 2011, http://www.youtube.com/watch?v=hkRELoqSQeQ

16   Vogt, Douglas B., "Final Analysis of President Obama's Certificate of Live Birth," June 13, 2011, accessed July 6, 2011, http://archiveindex.com/Obamas_certificate_of_Live_birth_June-12-2011_News_Release.pdf

17   Renshaw, Albert [orangegold1], "Obama Birth Certificate Faked In Adobe Illustrator - Official Proof 1 (Layers)," April 27, 2011, accessed July 6, 2011, http://www.youtube.com/watch?v=7s9StxsFllY

18   "Hello, my name is Albert Renshaw. I am 16 years old and in love with knowledge and understanding." – AlbertRenshaw.com, last updated March 4, 2011, accessed July 6, 2011, http://albertrenshaw.com/

19   "Alex Jones (radio host)," Wikipedia, accessed July 6, 2011, http://en.wikipedia.org/wiki/Alex_Jones_(radio_host)

20   "TheAlexJonesChannel's Channel," YouTube, accessed July 6, 2011, http://www.youtube.com/user/TheAlexJonesChannel#p/u

21   eCompConsultants.com, accessed July 6, 2011, http://www.ecompconsultants.com/consultants_zatkovich.php

22   Zatkovich, Ivan, "Analysis of Obama Birth Certificate PDF," April 29, 2011, accessed July 6, 2011, http://www.ecompconsultants.com/news/Obama-report.pdf

23   "About Dr. Neal Krawetz," accessed July 6, 2011, http://www.hackerfactor.com/about.php

24   Krawetz, Neal, "After Birth," April 28, 2011, accessed July 6, 2011, http://www.hackerfactor.com/blog/index.php?/archives/428-After-Birth.html

25   "National Review," Wikipedia, accessed July 6, 2011, http://en.wikipedia.org/wiki/National_Review

26   Goulding, Nathan, "PDF Layers in Obama's Birth Certificate," April 27, 2011, accessed July 6, 2011, http://www.nationalreview.com/corner/265767/pdf-layers-obamas-birth-certificate-nathan-goulding

27   Davidson, Kevin [Dr. Conspiracy], "Reply to Douglas Vogt (Updated)," May 31, 2011, accessed July 6, 2011, http://www.obamaconspiracy.org/2011/05/reply-to-douglas-vogt/

28   "Visitor Guide," Obama Conspiracy Theories, accessed July 6, 2011, http://www.obamaconspiracy.org/visitor-guide/

29   Corsi, Jerome R., "Expert: Obama doc is 'proof' – of fraud," WorldNetDaily, June 7, 2011, accessed July 6, 2011, http://www.wnd.com/?pageId=308397

30   Corsi, Jerome R., "Adobe expert doubts Obama birth certificate," WorldNetDaily, June 24, 2011, accessed July 10, 2011, http://www.wnd.com/?pageId=314717

31   Corsi, Jerome R., "Adobe book editor positive: Obama certificate is phony," WorldNetDaily, June 28, 2011, accessed July 10, 2011, http://www.wnd.com/?pageId=316749

32   Corsi, Jerome R., "Layered colors 'simple proof' of Obama document forgery," WorldNetDaily, July 26, 2011, accessed August 4, 2011, http://www.wnd.com/?pageId=326565

33 "Jerome Corsi: White House Running Scared Over Latest Discovery of Obama's True Origins 1/3" (Jerome R. Corsi interview with Alex Jones), 4:57, accessed July 6, 2011, http://www.youtube.com/user/TheAlexJonesChannel#p/u/460/BygadqqiFH8

34 It's possible that they might also release a low-quality forgery image *derived* from the high-quality forgery, but that's not what anybody has claimed in regard to the birth certificate. Nor has anyone shown the existence of any high-quality, layered document that the Adobe PDF *could* have been derived from.

   Neither has anyone proposed how we might get from some (theoretical) high-quality layered document to a lower-quality layered document, *and still have the layers of the lower-quality document keep the evidence of forgery.*

35 A high resolution copy of the "white-background" image has been available from the web site of the Worcester, Massachusetts Telegram & Gazette, at: http://www.telegram.com/apps/pbcsi.dll/bilde?Site=WT&Date=20110427 &Category=NEWS&ArtNo=110429737&Ref=V2&title=1 (accessed July 6, 2011).

   And an even higher resolution file is posted by Obama Conspiracy Theories at http://www.obamaconspiracy.org/wp-content/uploads/2011/06/ BirthCertificateHighResolution.jpg.

36 Guthrie, Savannah, online comment, accessed July 6, 2011, http://lockerz.com/ s/96540721. The second photo was posted to: http://lockerz.com/s/96540937

37 Why not scanned directly into the computer? A direct scan almost certainly would've picked up the safety-paper background. Hence, our conclusion that the original document seems to been photocopied first, and then scanned or photographed.

38 The Chicago Sun-Times, for example, at http://www.suntimes.com/news/ politics/obama/5048997-418/barack-obama-releases-long-form-birth-certificate- decries-silliness.html (accessed July 6, 2011)

39 "Obama releases detailed U.S. birth certificate," MSNBC, video report (video and transcript), 3:45, April 27, 2011, accessed July 6, 2011, http://www.msnbc.msn.com/id/42779923/ns/politics-white_house/

40 Renshaw, Albert [orangegold1], "Obama Birth Certificate Faked In Adobe Illustrator - Official Proof 1 (Layers)," 3:43, April 27, 2011, accessed July 6, 2011, http://www.youtube.com/watch?v=7s9StxsFllY

41 JPG or JPEG is the format most used for photos on the internet. It's also the standard electronic format used by almost all digital cameras.

42 Goulding, Nathan, "PDF Layers in Obama's Birth Certificate," National Review Online, April 27, 2011, accessed July 12, 2011, http://www.nationalreview.com/ corner/265767/pdf-layers-obamas-birth-certificate-nathan-goulding

43 Krawetz, Neal, "After Birth," April 28, 2011, accessed July 6, 2011, http://www.hackerfactor.com/blog/index.php?/archives/428-After-Birth.html

44 This PDF was created on a Macintosh computer, using Mac OS X software which I personally do not have at this time.

45 The Child's Wonder Picture Book of Favourite Stories [in verse], accessed July 6, 2011, http://books.google.com/books?id=VSIOAAAAQAAJ&printsec=frontcover &source=gbs_ge_summary_r&cad=0#v=onepage&q&f=false

46 Corsi, Jerome R., "Dr. Corsi Reveals First Name of Birth Certificate Forger – 5/26/2011" (interview with Tom Tancredo), 14:50, May 26, 2011, accessed July 6, 2011, http://www.youtube.com/watch?v=hkRELoqSQeQ

47   Renshaw, Albert [orangegold1], "Obama Birth Certificate Faked In Adobe Illustrator - Official Proof 1 (Layers)," 6:15, April 27, 2011, accessed July 6, 2011, http://www.youtube.com/watch?v=7s9StxsFllY

48   Renshaw, Albert [orangegold1], "Obama Birth Certificate Faked In Adobe Illustrator - Official Proof 1 (Layers)," 4:30, April 27, 2011, accessed July 6, 2011, http://www.youtube.com/watch?v=7s9StxsFllY

49   Denninger, Karl, "Obama Birth Certificate Scam? 2011-04-27 Obama.mp4," 4:25, April 27, 2011, accessed July 6, 2011, http://www.youtube.com/watch?v=2eOfYwYyS_c

50   Denninger, Karl, "Obama Birth Certificate Scam? 2011-04-27 Obama.mp4," 6:05, April 27, 2011, accessed July 6, 2011, http://www.youtube.com/watch?v=2eOfYwYyS_c

51   Zatkovich, Ivan, "Analysis of Obama Birth Certificate PDF," p.7, April 29, 2011, accessed July 6, 2011, http://www.ecompconsultants.com/news/Obama-report.pdf

52   "3TruthSeeker33," "Final Proof: Obama Birth Certificate a Fake, a Forgery, $10,000 Challenge!" uploader comments, June 7, 2011, accessed July 6, 2011, http://www.youtube.com/watch?v=LvALmxLZQBA

53   Corsi, Jerome R., "Unveiled! Hawaii's 1961 long-form birth certificates," WorldNetDaily, July 28, 2009, accessed July 6, 2011, http://www.wnd.com/?pageId=105347

54   "Miss Tickly," "The Odds are Racist," Obama's Garden blog, May 2, 2011, accessed July 6, 2011, http://obamasgarden.wordpress.com/2011/05/02/the-odds-are-racist/

55   Renshaw, Albert [orangegold1], "Obama Birth Certificate Faked In Adobe Illustrator - Official Proof 4 (OCR / Optimizing)," 2:35, May 2, 2011, accessed July 6, 2011, http://www.youtube.com/watch?v=nW_PWzhgvDs

56   Renshaw, Albert [orangegold1], "Obama Birth Certificate Faked In Adobe Illustrator - Official Proof 4 (OCR / Optimizing)," 2:00, May 2, 2011, accessed July 6, 2011, http://www.youtube.com/watch?v=nW_PWzhgvDs

57   Vogt, Douglas B., "Revised and Expanded Affidavit," p. 6, May 22, 2011, accessed July 6, 2011, http://www.archiveindex.com/Obama_expanded_affidavit_5-22-2011.pdf

58   Corsi, Jerome R., "Layered colors 'simple proof' of Obama document forgery," July 26, 2011, accessed August 8, 2011, http://www.wnd.com/?pageId=326565

59   Corsi, Jerome R., Interview with Ed Hale, The Lion's Den, August 2, 2011, 34:15, accessed August 3, 2011, http://www.plainsradionetwork.com/PlainsRadio/8-2.html

60   Corsi, Jerome R., "Experts say Obama certificate not scan of original document," August 2, 2011, accessed August 8, 2011, http://www.wnd.com/?pageId=329221

61   Ibid.

62   http://archiveindex.com/Original_White_House_Certificate_of_Live_birth_long-form_4-27-2011.pdf. Accessed August 3, 2011.

63   Adobe Systems Inc., PDF Reference, p. 100, 2001, accessed August 8, 2011, http://partners.adobe.com/public/developer/en/pdf/PDFReference.pdf

64   timeanddate.com, accessed August 8, 2011, http://timeanddate.com/worldclock/meetingtime.html?month=4&day=27&year=2011&p1=0&p2=136&p3=263&p4=-1

65 Stein, Sam, "Obama Birth Certificate Released By White House," Huffington Post, April 27, 2011, accessed August 8, 2011, http://www.huffingtonpost.com/2011/04/27/obama-birth-certificate-r_n_854248.html

66 timeanddate.com, accessed August 8, 2011, http://timeanddate.com/worldclock/meetingtime.html?month=4&day=28&year=2011&p1=234&p2=263&p3=0&p4=0

67 For the sake of thoroughness, I'll mention here that Perkins Coie, the law firm of lawyer Judy Corley who flew to Hawaii to retrieve the birth certificates, has its head office in Seattle, Washington. However, while Corley handled the paper documents, she wouldn't have created the PDF. And even if she did, she's based in Washington, DC, not Seattle, so there's no reason for her computer to be on West Coast time. Douglas Vogt, on the other hand, is known to have handled the modified file. And we have no source for this file other than from his server.

68 These seven reasons are that the three characteristics we noted – that a) the item serves no purpose for a forger, b) the item would have cost time and effort, and c) the item would arouse suspicion and increase the risk of getting caught – *all* apply to each of the following items: 1) the badly-scrambled nature of the layers, 2) the division and "choice" of grayscaled and solid-color elements, 3) the white halo, 4) the duplicate letters – *most of which were elements of the form which would have been far easier scanned and left alone,* 5) the scaling, 6) the nature of the stamps, including their mixed-up nature and green color, and 7) the white dots.

69 Denninger, Karl, "2011-05-02 Final Birth Certificate," 1:35, May 2, 2011, accessed July 6, 2011, http://www.youtube.com/watch?v=85yVkL94_BU

70 This was uploaded to the web in 2008 by her brother James Coats, at http://passportsusa.com/?page_id=209

71 Corsi, Jerome R., "Obama birth certificate linked to previous 'forgery'?," WorldNetDaily, May 8, 2011, accessed July 6, 2011, http://www.wnd.com/?pageId=295109

72 "Hawaii Birth Certificate – 1963," June 18, 2008, accessed July 7, 2011, http://snarkybytes.com/2008/06/18/hawaii-birth-certificate-1963/

73 Corsi, Jerome R., "Dr. Corsi Reveals First Name of Birth Certificate Forger – 5/26/2011" (interview with Tom Tancredo), 14:05, May 26, 2011, accessed July 6, 2011, http://www.youtube.com/watch?v=hkRELoqSQeQ

74 Vogt, Douglas B., "Affidavit," p. 3, June 24, 2011, accessed July 6, 2011, http://archiveindex.com/Obama%20affidavit%206-24-2011.pdf

75 Denninger, Karl, "2011-05-17 Birth Cert Smoking Gun.mp4," 2:00, May 17, 2011, accessed on July 6, 2011, http://www.youtube.com/watch?v=haiRCLItdEQ&feature=relmfu

76 Denninger, Karl, "Tickerguy: 1, ObaBots: 0," April 29, 2011, accessed July 7, 2011, http://market-ticker.org/akcs-www?singlepost=2530047

77 "Hawaii Birth Certificate – 1963," June 18, 2008, accessed July 7, 2011, http://snarkybytes.com/2008/06/18/hawaii-birth-certificate-1963/

78 "Jerome Corsi: White House Running Scared Over Latest Discovery of Obama's True Origins 1/3" (Jerome R. Corsi interview with Alex Jones), 13:05, May 20, 2011, accessed July 6, 2011, http://www.youtube.com/user/TheAlexJonesChannel#p/u/460/BygadqqiFH8

79   Corsi, Jerome R., "Criminal complaint details birth-certificate 'forgery'," WorldNetDaily, June 5, 2011, accessed July 10, 2011, http://www.wnd.com/?pageId=306953

80   Vogt, Douglas B., "Final Analysis of President Obama's Certificate of Live Birth," June 13, 2011, p. 12, accessed July 7, 2011, http://archiveindex.com/Obamas_certificate_of_Live_birth_June-12-2011_News_Release.pdf

81   *Ibid.*, pp. 11 – 12.

82   Corsi, Jerome R., "'The Obama code': Hidden messages in birth document?" May 21, 2011, accessed July 7, 2011, http://www.wnd.com/?pageId=301329

83   This was made available at: http://www.whitehouse.gov/sites/default/files/rss_viewer/birth-certificate-correspondence.pdf

84   "Frequently Asked Questions about Vital Records of President Barack Hussein Obama II," Hawaii Department of Health, accessed July 7, 2011, http://hawaii.gov/health/vital-records/obama.html

85   Isikoff, Michael, "Ex-Hawaii official denounces 'ludicrous' birther claims," NBC News, April 11, 2011, accessed July 7, 2011, http://www.msnbc.msn.com/id/42519951/ns/politics-more_politics/t/ex-hawaii-official-denounces-ludicrous-birther-claims/

86   "From A to Z: What's wrong with Obama's birth certificate?" WorldNetDaily, May 13, 2011, accessed July 7, 2011, http://www.wnd.com/?pageId=296881

87   Corsi, Jerome R., "Unveiled! Hawaii's 1961 long-form birth certificates," WorldNetDaily, July 28, 2009, accessed July 6, 2011, http://www.wnd.com/?pageId=105347

88   Bennett, Charles G. and Tokuyama,"Vital Records in Hawaii," Hawaii Medical Journal, Vol. 15 , No. 2 – November-December 1955, posted at http://www.wnd.com/files/CHARLESBENNETT.pdf, accessed July 7, 2011.

89   "Jerome Corsi: White House Running Scared Over Latest Discovery of Obama's True Origins 1/3" (Jerome R. Corsi interview with Alex Jones), 12:08, May 20, 2011, accessed July 7, 2011, http://www.youtube.com/user/TheAlexJonesChannel#p/u/460/BygadqqiFH8

90   Corsi, Jerome R., "Nordyke numbers expose Obama document fraud?" WorldNetDaily, May 16, 2011, accessed July 7, 2011, http://www.wnd.com/?pageId=299781

91   Bennett, Charles G. and Tokuyama,"Vital Records in Hawaii," Hawaii Medical Journal, Vol. 15 , No. 2 – November-December 1955, posted at http://www.wnd.com/files/CHARLESBENNETT.pdf, accessed July 7, 2011.

92   Tuchmann, Gary, "CNN investigation: Obama born in U.S.," CNN, April 25, 2011, 1:55, accessed July 7, 2011, http://www.cnn.com/2011/POLITICS/04/25/birthers.obama.hawaii/index.html?hpt=C1

93   The screenshot link referenced was: http://i54.tinypic.com/2ze08wo.jpg

94   "Do you have a question for Dr. Jerome Corsi, author of Where's the Birth Certificate? Please post it here," June 3, 2011, accessed July 7, 2011, http://conservativewarriorprincess.com/wordpressblog/2011/06/03/do-you-have-a-question-for-dr-jerome-corsi-author-of-wheres-the-birth-certificate-please-post-it-here/

95 "Where's the Birth Certificate: Special Guest Jerome Corsi," The Teri O'Brien Show, June 5, 2011, accessed July 7, 2011, http://www.blogtalkradio.com/teri-obrien/2011/06/05/the-teri-obrien-show

96 Davidson, Kevin [Dr. Conspiracy], "Obama's birth certificate number,"April 29, 2011, accessed July 7, 2011, http://www.obamaconspiracy.org/2011/04/obamas-birth-certificate-number/

97 "Researcher," "Research Summary on Hawaii Birth Certificate Number 151-1961-010641: Where Did the Number Come From?" The Post & Email, May 13, 2011, accessed July 7, 2011, http://www.thepostemail.com/2011/05/13/research-summary-on-hawaii-birth-certificate-number-151-1961-010641/. The theory was also reported on by Corsi and WorldNetDaily, at: http://www.wnd.com/?pageId=300201

98 Report of the Panel to Evaluate the U.S. Standard Certificates, April 2000, U.S. Division of Vital Statistics, accessed July 7, 2011, http://www.cdc.gov/nchs/data/dvs/panelreport_acc.pdf

99 Corsi, Jerome R., "Expert: Obama doc is 'proof' – of fraud," June 7, 2011, accessed July 7, 2011, http://www.wnd.com/?pageId=308397

100 Characters which occur once and are therefore left out include &, 6, G, 0 (zero), w, f, 2, T, L, Y, D, M and W.

101 We ought to note that we have generally considered the AP document to be higher quality than the PDF, and have relied on this fact for some of our conclusions. But a review shows that the small vertical ripple-zone distortions won't affect any of those.

102 For comparison, the PDF and high-resolution AP images are available from: http://www.whitehouse.gov/sites/default/files/rss_viewer/birth-certificate-long-form.pdf and http://www.obamaconspiracy.org/wp-content/uploads/2011/06/BirthCertificateHighResolution.jpg.

103 Many thanks to "The Right Reverend Theodore Munk" for his excellent compilation of 332 different contemporary type styles by apparently every major manufacturer of typewriters: Adler, Facit, Hermes, IBM, Olivetti, Olympia, R.C. Allen, Remington, Royal, and Smith Corona. Munk's compilation, from the 1964 National Office Machine Dealers' Association Blue Book, was accessed at: http://munk.org/typecast/2011/04/23/1964-nomda-blue-book-adler-typewriter-font-styles/

104 "Hawaii Birth Certificate – 1963," June 18, 2008, accessed July 7, 2011, http://snarkybytes.com/2008/06/18/hawaii-birth-certificate-1963/

105 Corsi, Jerome R., "Expert: Obama doc is 'proof' – of fraud," June 7, 2011, accessed July 7, 2011, http://www.wnd.com/?pageId=308397

106 After completing this chapter, I learned that Mr. Irey has stated that he "knew it was a forgery" before he even looked at it. He claims to have been told by a friend with a Secret Service contact that "there was no birth certificate in the records." ("Paul Irey's biased analysis - 'I knew it was a forgery before I even looked at it'," June 25, 2011, accessed July 10, 2011, http://rcradioshow.blogspot.com/2011/06/paul-ireys-biased-analysis-i-knew-it.html. See the accompanying audio, RC Radio 6-23-2011, with interviews of Linton Mohammed and Paul Irey, beginning about 72:10.)

107 "Jerome Corsi: White House Running Scared Over Latest Discovery of Obama's True Origins 1/3" (Jerome R. Corsi interview with Alex Jones), 8:53, May 20, 2011, accessed July 6, 2011, http://www.youtube.com/user/TheAlexJonesChannel#p/u/460/BygadqqiFH8

108 Corsi, Jerome R., "'The Obama code': Hidden messages in birth document?" May 21, 2011, accessed July 7, 2011, http://www.wnd.com/?pageId=301329

109 "Unmasking the Face on Mars," NASA, May 24, 2001, accessed July 7, 2011, http://science.nasa.gov/science-news/science-at-nasa/2001/ast24may_1/

110 Corsi, Jerome R., "Dr. Corsi Reveals First Name of Birth Certificate Forger – 5/26/2011" (interview with Tom Tancredo), 17:05, May 26, 2011, accessed July 7, 2011, http://www.youtube.com/watch?v=hkRELoqSQeQ

111 Corsi, Jerome R., "Unveiled! Hawaii's 1961 long-form birth certificates," WorldNetDaily, July 28, 2009, accessed July 6, 2011, http://www.wnd.com/?pageId=105347

112 "Scrubbed again! Obama's hospital doctor changed," WorldNetDaily, May 8, 2011, accessed July 7, 2011, http://www.wnd.com/?pageId=295265

113 Voell, Paula, "Teacher from Kenmore recalls Obama was a focused student," The Buffalo News, January 20, 2009, accessed July 7, 2011, http://mysite.ncnetwork.net/res1002yg/obama/Teacher%20from%20Kenmore%20recalls%20Obama%20was%20a%20focused%20student%20%20Don't%20Miss%20%20The%20Buffalo%20News.htm

114 "Where's the Birth Certificate: Special Guest Jerome Corsi," The Teri O'Brien Show, 31:10, June 5, 2011, accessed July 7, 2011, http://www.blogtalkradio.com/teri-obrien/2011/06/05/the-teri-obrien-show

115 "Summary of the HIPAA Privacy Rule," United States Department of Health and Human Services, p. 4, accessed July 7, 2011, http://www.hhs.gov/ocr/privacy/hipaa/understanding/summary/privacysummary.pdf

116 *Ibid.,* p. 18.

117 Henig, Jess, "Born in the U.S.A.," FactCheck.org, August 21, 2008, accessed July 7, 2011, http://factcheck.org/2008/08/born-in-the-usa/

118 "Results of Drinking Water Tests for Chromium VI Available to the Public," Hawaii Department of Health News Release, January 25, 2011, accessed July 7, 2011, http://hawaii.gov/health/about/pr/2011/11-005.pdf

119 Bennett, Charles G. and Tokuyama,"Vital Records in Hawaii," Hawaii Medical Journal, Vol. 15 , No. 2 – November-December 1955, posted at http://www.wnd.com/files/CHARLESBENNETT.pdf, accessed July 7, 2011.

120 Barack Obama official long-form birth certificate, posted by the White House on April 27, 2011, accessed July 7, 2011, http://www.whitehouse.gov/sites/default/files/rss_viewer/birth-certificate-long-form.pdf

121 "Barack Hussein Obama Sr. Immigration File," provided by Heather Smathers, a reporter for the Arizona Indpendent, accessed July 7, 2011, http://www.scribd.com/doc/54015762/Barack-Hussein-Obama-Sr-Immigration-File

122 Corsi, Jerome R., "Did Obama's father forget when he was born?" WorldNetDaily, June 2, 2011, accessed July 9, 2011, http://www.wnd.com/?pageId=306653

123 Smathers, Heather, "EXCLUSIVE: Dad's Immigration File Offers More Evidence Of Obama's Birthplace," Arizona Independent, April 27, 2011, accessed on July 7, 2011, http://www2.az-independent.com/?p=2974

124 "Barack Obama: Mother not just a girl from Kansas," Chicago Tribune, March 27, 2007, accessed July 7, 2011, http://www.chicagotribune.com/news/politics/obama/chi-0703270151mar27-archive,0,5853572,full.story

125 "World Map 1960" (zoomable), National Geographic, accessed July 7, 2011, http://www.maps.com/map.aspx?pid=15933

126 This was uploaded to the web in 2008 by her brother James Coats, at
     http://passportsusa.com/?page_id=209

127 "1961 Hawaii Department of Health Registrar Identified! – Updated!" July 18, 2011,
     We the People of the United States blog, accessed July 20, 2011,
     https://wtpotus.wordpress.com/2011/07/18/1961-hawaii-department-of-health-
     registrar-identified/#more-10901. A search that same day at Intelius.com found a
     Verna K. Lee in Honolulu, aged 94; so it appears Ms. Lee would've been in her 40s.

128 Klein, Aaron, "Was young Obama Indonesian citizen?" WorldNetDaily, August 17,
     2008, accessed July 7, 2011, http://www.wnd.com/?pageId=72656

129 "It has long been a recognized principle in this country that, if a child born here is
     taken during minority to the country of his parents' origin, where his parents resume
     their former allegiance, he does not thereby lose his citizenship in the United States
     provided that, on attaining majority, he elects to retain that citizenship and to return
     to the United States to assume its duties." *Perkins v. Elg*, United States Supreme
     Court, 1939, referenced on July 7, 2011 via http://supreme.justia.com/us/307/325/

130 FightTheSmears.com included in their page on Obama's citizenship and birth
     certificate the following quote from FactCheck.org: "When Barack Obama Jr. was
     born on Aug. 4,1961, in Honolulu, Kenya was a British colony, still part of the United
     Kingdom's dwindling empire. As a Kenyan native, Barack Obama Sr. was a British
     subject whose citizenship status was governed by The British Nationality Act of 1948.
     That same act governed the status of Obama Sr.'s children. Since Sen. Obama has
     neither renounced his U.S. citizenship nor sworn an oath of allegiance to Kenya, his
     Kenyan citizenship automatically expired on Aug. 4,1982." (http://web.archive.org/
     web/20081002140331/http://fightthesmears.com/articles/5/birthcertificate).

     The site has a label at the bottom: "Paid for by Obama for America." The domain
     registrant for FightTheSmears.com is Obama for America, 233 N. Michigan Ave, Apt
     2416, Chicago, Illinois 60601. *Obama for America* is the official Obama campaign
     organization.

131 The question, of course, is important to whether Obama is eligible to be President.

132 Knott, Alex, "Obama Campaign Racks Up Large Legal Fees," Roll Call, March 31,
     2011, accessed July 7, 2011, http://www.rollcall.com/issues/56_103/Obama-
     Campaign-Racks-Up-Large-Legal-Fees-204489-1.html

133 The Federal Election Commission database shows fundraising of nearly $779 million
     for Obama, versus $384 million for McCain. http://query.nictusa.com/cgi-
     bin/cancomsrs/?_08+00+PR, accessed July 7, 2011.

134 "Birther Scorecard," an anonymous (pro-Obama) "scorecard" of lawsuits related to
     Barack Obama's Presidential eligibility, last updated February 2, 2011, accessed July
     7, 2011, http://tesibria.typepad.com/whats_your_evidence/BIRTHER%20CASE
     %20LIST.pdf

135 *Berg v. Obama* was filed on August 21, 2008, and dismissed in October 2008. Berg
     bypassed the United States Court of Appeals for the 3rd Circuit, and filed a petition
     (several times) with the United States Supreme Court, which was denied each time.
     In November 2009, the United States Court of Appeals affirmed the district court's
     ruling that Berg lacked standing.

     Hollister v. Soetoro was filed on March 5, 2009, and was dismissed. The Court of
     Appeals upheld the dismissal, and the United States Supreme Court declined to hear
     an appeal.

Keyes v. Bowen was filed on November 14, 2008. Obama's lawyers filed a motion to quash the subpeona, and the case was dismissed. The California Court of Appeal affirmed the dismissal on October 25, 2010, and the California Supreme Court declined to review the case on February 2, 2011.

Source: http://en.wikipedia.org/wiki/Barack_Obama_presidential_eligibility_litigation, accessed July 7, 2011.

136   All of the named cases allege that even if Mr. Obama were proven to be born in the United States, he would have lost his status as an American natural born citizen upon going to Indonesia as a child and receiving Indonesian citizenship.

Hollister v. Soetoro: "...Soetoro is an Indonesian citizen, and therefore he is not eligible to be President of the United States... As a result of Soetoro's Indonesian 'natural' citizenship status, Soetoro could never regain U.S. 'natural born' status, if he in fact he ever held such, which we doubt." (http://www.scribd.com/doc/9934967/Berg-Hollister-v-Soetoro-aka-Obama-Biden-Complaint, accessed July 8, 2011)

Berg v. Obama: "Even if Obama was, in fact, born in Hawaii, he lost his U.S. citizenship when his mother re-married and moved to Indonesia with her Indonesian husband." (http://docs.justia.com/cases/federal/district-courts/pennsylvania/paedce/2:2008cv04083/281573/13/0.pdf, accessed July 8, 2011)

Keyes v. Bowen: "In the litigation against Senator Obama, allegations have been made that his admitted dual citizenship in Indonesia, and lack of evidence that he renounced the same, caused a loss of his United States Citizenship as a matter of law." (http://www.scribd.com/doc/8980887/Keyes-v-Bowen, accessed July 8, 2011)

137   Kovacs, Joe, "Hawaii elections clerk: Obama not born here," June 10, 2010, accessed July 8, 2011, http://www.wnd.com/?pageId=165041

138   Corsi, Jerome R., "Hawaii official now swears: No Obama birth certificate," January 24, 2011, accessed July 8, 2011, http://www.wnd.com/?pageId=254401

139   Weigel, David, "Honolulu city clerk debunks new 'birther' theory," June 21, 2010, accessed July 8, 2011, http://voices.washingtonpost.com/right-now/2010/06/there_are_some_people_who.html

140   "Tim Adams, Senior Elections Clerk," The Fogbow, accessed July 8, 2011, http://www.thefogbow.com/special-reports/tim-adams

141   Kovacs, Joe, "Hawaii governor announces 'exact' place of Obama birth," May 5, 2010, WorldNetDaily, accessed July 8, 2011, http://www.wnd.com/?pageId=150125

142   "Obama's Birth Certificate Verified By State," KITV, November 1, 2008, accessed July 8, 2011, http://www.kitv.com/r/17860890/detail.html

143   "Hawai'i Health Department Grants President Obama's Request for Certified Copies of 'Long Form' Birth Certificate," State of Hawaii Press Release, April 27, 2011, accessed July 8, 2011, http://hawaii.gov/health/vital-records/News_Release_Birth_Certificate_042711.pdf

144   *Ibid.*

145   "Mike Evans: Hawaii Guv Neil Abercrombie told me NO Obama Birth Certificate in Hawaii – 1/20/11," 1:25, January 20, 2011, uploaded January 24, 2011, accessed July 8, 2011, http://www.youtube.com/watch?v=GD0U_j02jQE

146   Winter, Jana, "Celebrity Journalist: I Never Spoke to Hawaii Gov About Obama Birth Certificate," January 26, 2011, accessed July 8, 2011, http://www.foxnews.com/politics/2011/01/26/celebrity-journalist-says-he-never-talked-hawaii-governor-obama-birth/

147 "Mike Evans Backtracks Comments On Obama's Missing Birth Certificate – 1/26/11," the Peter Boyles Show, 26:40, January 26, 2011, accessed July 8, 2011, http://www.youtube.com/watch?v=PBb7loS_3r4

148 Winter, Jana, "Celebrity Journalist: I Never Spoke to Hawaii Gov About Obama Birth Certificate," January 26, 2011, accessed July 8, 2011, http://www.foxnews.com/ politics/2011/01/26/celebrity-journalist-says-he-never-talked-hawaii-governor-obama-birth/

149 Corsi, Jerome R., "Hawaii governor can't find Obama birth certificate," WorldNetDaily, January 18, 2011, accessed July 8, 2011, http://www.wnd.com/? pageId=252833

150 "'This is a collaborative endeavor'," Honolulu Star-Advertiser, January 18, 2011, accessed July 8, 2011, http://www.staradvertiser.com/editorials/20110118_ This_is_a_collaborative_endeavor.html

151 Williams, J.B., "The Theory is Now a Conspiracy And Facts Don't Lie," Canada Free Press, September 10, 2009, accessed July 9, 2011, http://www.canadafreepress.com/2009/williams091209.htm

152 Williams, J.B., "The Theory is Now a Conspiracy—II," Canada Free Press, September 15, 2009, accessed July 9, 2011, http://canadafreepress.com/index.php/article/14741

153 *Ibid.*

154 Williams, J.B., "DNC Failed to Certify Obama as Eligible in MOST States!" Canada Free Press, September 25, 2009, accessed July 9, 2011, http://canadafreepress.com/index.php/article/15127

155 Bernstein, David, "The Speech," Chicago Magazine, June 2007, accessed July 9, 2011, http://www.chicagomag.com/Chicago-Magazine/June-2007/The-Speech/

156 There's no computer font that would give authentic-looking variation of typed characters. Therefore, images of real typed characters would've been used. And these most likely would have been taken from other birth certificates.

157 As of August 2011, *WorldNetDaily* continues to bring forth new witnesses, both anonymous and named, to give opinions that the birth certificate is forged. The "cut-off point" for this book is roughly 3 months after the release of the long-form certificate. By that point in time, most of the new witnesses seem to be relying mostly on issues that we've dealt with. This is an indication that there probably aren't very many new arguments available.

158 "Dr Jerome Corsi on Birth certificate layers," uploaded May 22, 2011, accessed July 9, 2011, http://www.youtube.com/watch?v=kGlqGrwgAGY

159 Corsi, Jerome R., "Criminal complaint charges Obama birth record 'forged'," WorldNetDaily, May 31, 2011, accessed July 9, 2011, http://www.wnd.com/? pageId=305705

160 Corsi, Jerome R., "Adobe book editor positive: Obama certificate is phony," WorldNetDaily, June 28, 2011, accessed July 9, 2011, http://www.wnd.com/? pageId=316749

161 Corsi, Jerome R., "Criminal complaint details birth-certificate 'forgery'," WorldNetDaily, June 5, 2011, accessed July 9, 2011, http://www.wnd.com/? pageId=306953

162 Corsi, Jerome R., "Adobe expert doubts Obama birth certificate," WorldNetDaily, June 24, 2011, http://www.wnd.com/?pageId=314717

163 Corsi, Jerome R., "Criminal complaint charges Obama birth record 'forged'," WorldNetDaily, May 31, 2011, accessed July 9, 2011, http://www.wnd.com/?pageId=305705

164 An anonymous "prominent software engineer" quoted by Dr. Jerome Corsi claims that the "unham Obama" portion of the signature is too perfectly aligned to be authentic. Again, a close examination of the documents shows that this isn't the case. The writer completely ignores, by the way, the "Ann" portion of the signature, which dips so far down it touches the line. And even the portion mentioned, while well-aligned, is irregular in its formation of characters and in their height above the line. (Corsi, Jerome R., "Mathematical 'proof' Obama birth certificate a forgery," WorldNetDaily, July 5, 2011, accessed July 10, 2011, http://www.wnd.com/?pageId=319221)

165 Corsi, Jerome R., "New 'birth certificate' anomalies inexplicable," WorldNetDaily, May 13, 2011, accessed July 9, 2011, http://www.wnd.com/?pageId=298101

166 Corsi, Jerome R., "Hawaii official now swears: No Obama birth certificate," January 24, 2011, accessed July 8, 2011, http://www.wnd.com/?pageId=254401

167 "Eligibility hits New York airwaves," WorldNetDaily, May 17, 2011, accessed July 10, 2011, http://www.wnd.com/?pageId=299921

168 Experts Doubt The Authenticity of Obama's Birth Certificate, Tea Party Power Hour (Mark Gillar), 94:30, July 31, 2011, accessed August 10, 2011, http://www.blogtalkradio.com/markgillar/2011/07/31/experts-debate-the-authenticity-of-obamas-birth-certificate

169 In fact, a restrictive Google search on "+'alex jones' +'9/11 truther'," on July 22, 2011, produced "About 455,000 results."

170 "Dr. Corsi Reveals First Name of Birth Certificate Forger – 5/26/2011" (interview with Tom Tancredo), 18:40, May 26, 2011, accessed July 6, 2011, http://www.youtube.com/watch?v=hkRELoqSQeQ

171 Press briefing by White House Press Secretary Robert Gibbs, May 27, 2009. As of July 9, 2011, a copy of the video was available at: http://citizensagainstproobamamediabias.wordpress.com/2009/05/30/robert-gibbs-lies-about-barrys-birth-certificate/

172 Shane, Leo, "'Birther' sentenced to six months in prison, kicked out of Army," Stars and Stripes, December 15, 2010, accessed July 10, 2011, http://www.stripes.com/news/birther-sentenced-to-six-months-in-prison-kicked-out-of-army-1.128924

173 "American Patriot Foundation: FTC Terry Lakin Defense Fund," March 30, 2010, accessed July 10, 2011, http://www.youtube.com/watch?v=ea9JVnck_-E&feature=related

174 "Response to the Release of the Barack Obama Birth Certificate from the Terry Lakin Action Fund," April 27, 2011, accessed July 10, 2011, http://www.terrylakinactionfund.com/obamaresponse.html

175 "Chris Matthews: Why Doesn't Obama Just Release The Birth Certificate," Hardball With Chris Matthews, MSNBC, uploaded to YouTube December 27, 2010, accessed July 10, 2011, http://www.youtube.com/watch?v=8VTMWRpkVbI

WOULD YOU LIKE TO RECEIVE UPDATES OR BE NOTIFIED OF FUTURE PUBLICATIONS BY JOHN WOODMAN?

If you'd like to read the latest news, get free updates on the Obama birth certificate issue, and be notified of future publications by John Woodman, please visit our web site at *www.ObamaBirthBook.com.* Sign up on the "Get Updates!" page. Or, drop us an email at:

johnwoodmanauthor@springfieldcomputerguy.com

We respect your privacy and will use your email address only to send birth certificate updates and notify you of new works from the author. We won't sell or give your email address to anybody else – and you may unsubscribe at any time.

Media Requests

The author is available for media interviews. Please contact us at: *media@obamabirthbook.com.*

Discounts for Bulk Purchases

For information on discounts for bulk purchases of this book, please contact us at: *discounts@obamabirthbook.com.*

Made in the USA
Las Vegas, NV
08 September 2022

54902461R00138